Forty Masses
with
Young People

DONAL NEARY, SJ

Forty Masses
with
Young People

XXIII
TWENTY-THIRD PUBLICATIONS
Mystic, Connecticut
and
the columba press
Dublin, Ireland

Acknowledgements

The publisher acknowledges the permission of the following to quote from copyright material: Jerusalem Bible is copyright © 1966, 1968, Darton, Longman & Todd Ltd and Doubleday & Co Inc; The New Revised Standard Version is copyright © 1989, Division of Christian Education of the National Council of Churches of Christ in the United States of America; The Grail Psalms are copyright © 1963, The Grail (England); John Harriot and *The Tablet* for the quotation on page 26; Silvester O'Flynn OFMCap for the quotation on page 34; *The Furrow* for the quotation from Peter Lemass on page 87; William Johnston SJ and Wm Collins & Son for the quotation on page 131; Sheila Cassidy and Darton, Longman & Todd for the quotation on page 152. Unattributed communion reflections are by the author.

Published simultaneously by

The Columba Press
93 The Rise, Mount Merrion,
Blackrock, Co Dublin
ISBN 1 85607 107 3

and

Twenty-Third Publications
185 Willow Street
P.O. Box 180
Mystic, CT 06355
(203) 536-2611
800-321-0411

ISBN 0-89622-630-1
Library of Congress Catalog Card Number

Contents

THEMES: CARE FOR THE WORLD

Forty Masses
with
Young People

Introduction

Forty Masses with Young People presents Masses suitable for young people 16-25 years of age and older. Masses for feasts of the liturgical year are included, along with Masses on themes which are of immediate interest and concern to young people.

These Masses take into account the spiritual development and interest of the 16-25 age group, and are composed for use in schools, religious education programs, youth groups, and at times when a priest or teacher may want to give a group some help in preparing a liturgy as well as on retreats, and on days of reflection. Like most youth resources, they may be used also with older age groups.

The readings and prayers in these Masses attempt to present an integral approach to liturgical themes. Relationship with God, the Christian way of life, a concern with justice, and with relationships with others are all presented for prayer and reflection. In this way a presentation of liturgical themes is faithful both to the whole Gospel and to the needs of young people today.

Using This Book
This book is best used by priests, teachers and young people together. They may select a theme themselves, or may even pick and choose between readings from different themes. Like any liturgical book, it may be adapted to the age and the level of understanding of the group. The book is for the people, not the people for the book.

The *Introduction* should be read by a young person, not by the priest if possible. Preparation, as in all liturgical reading, is necessary, as the text is written to be spoken. It is best to work from the principle that everything read at a liturgy should be prepared beforehand. A link is made in the *Introduction* between the theme of the day and the life and message of Jesus.

The *Penitential Rite* sometimes uses texts from *The Roman Missal;* other times, newly-composed texts.

Readings are chosen with reference to the theme or the feast. A priest or other leader of the group using these readings needs to reflect over them beforehand, so that the homily or any other presentation after the Gospel (e.g. meditation or drama) makes the link between the readings and the theme.

Personal and prayerful reflection from a priest or teacher is particularly relevant in a young age group. A *Communion Reflection* is offered; this needs careful preparation. Communion reflections are enhanced by this careful preparation, and also by slow and practiced reading.

The *Alleluia* verse has been omitted, following the recommendation of *The Roman Missal* that it is better to omit it when it is not being sung.

I wish to thank the staff and students of Mater Dei Institute of Education, Dublin, for their contribution to this book, which has been born largely out of the college's vibrant liturgical life.

Donal Neary SJ

1. Advent

Introduction

We see in Mary a woman of faith: she put her whole life on the line for God who asked her to be the mother of Jesus. She is also a woman who made a very strong choice for God in her life, whose vocation, like ours, was to bring Christ to the world. She is the one who now lives with God as we one day hope to: fully alive in the love and in the life of eternity. Our Mass today is our remembrance of her and also our trust in her help, that she can help us by her prayers. We'll think in the Mass mainly of her faith and trust in God as she brought Jesus into the world. She was his first teacher; maybe in this Mass we can pray especially for our families.

Penitential Rite

As we begin our Mass we recall that we are sinful and selfish; that we need the forgiveness of God and of each other in our lives. We particularly ask God's forgiveness for our neglect of our families and for any ways in which we unnecessarily cause them hurt, harm or pain. We ask pardon, too, for neglect of faith and of ways in which we have been arrogant and self-indulgent.

Lord Jesus, you are Son of God and Son of Mary:
Lord have mercy. R.
Lord Jesus, you have come to save sinners:
Christ have mercy. R.
Lord Jesus, you plead for us with our Father in heaven:
Lord have mercy. R.

Opening Prayer

God our Father, we see in Mary, the mother of your Son,
a person, like us in all but sin,
who welcomed your call in her life to be mother of your Son.
We ask that we be helped by her example and her prayers
to bring Jesus to birth again and again in our world
as we try to live lives in the spirit of his Gospel.
We ask this through Christ our Lord. Amen.

First Reading *Isaiah 9:1,5-7*

Because of the response of Mary to God, the light of God, Jesus Christ entered into the world. This passage of the bible was one Mary would have read many times herself, as she pondered on her own calling by God – the promise of God to send Christ into the world.

A reading from the prophet Isaiah.

The people that walked in darkness
have seen a great light.
On those who live in a land of deep shadow
a light has shone.
You have made their gladness greater,
you have made their joy increase.
For there is a child born for us
a son given to us
and dominion is laid on his shoulders;
and this is the name they give him:
Wonder-Counsellor, Mighty-God,
Eternal-Father, Prince of Peace.
Wide is his dominion
in a peace that has no end.
From this time onwards and forever
the love of the Lord God will do this.

Responsorial Psalm
Psalm 99 This is a joyful song of praise to our God.
RESPONSE: The word was made flesh and lived among us.

Cry out with joy to the Lord all the earth,
serve the Lord with gladness,
Come before him, singing for joy. R.

Know that the Lord is God,
he made us, we belong to him,
We are his people, the sheep of his flock. R.

Go within his gates giving thanks,
enter his courts with songs of joy,
give thanks to him and bless his name. R.

Gospel *John 19:25-27*
The faith and love of Mary for Jesus and his apostles are seen in her presence at the foot of the Cross. It shows her as a woman of courage, who didn't try to escape the hard experiences of life and love. She was there when she was needed; she followed through to the end her choice to love and serve God.

A reading from the holy Gospel according to John.

Near the cross of Jesus stood his mother and his mother's sister, Mary the wife of Clopas, and Mary of Magdala. Seeing his mother and the disciple he loved standing near her, Jesus said to his mother, 'Woman, this is your son.' Then to the disciple Jesus said, 'This is your mother.' And from that moment the disciple made a place for her in his home.

Prayer of the Faithful
Let us make our prayers to God, remembering people we want to pray for, especially our families.

We pray for our parents, brothers and sisters, for all in our families who may be in trouble or sickness, that God may be close to them and bless them. R.
Response: Lord, be gracious and bless us.
We pray for families who are in trouble through lack of employment or decent housing, for families in whom there are conflicts and poor relationships, that they may be helped by others who see their needs. R.
For any of our family who have died, that God may welcome them home and comfort those who miss them. R.
We pray that we may follow Mary's example, growing strong in faith and in love, asking for the courage to follow God's call in our lives. R.
We pray now through Mary's intercession
that we may be helped in our lives by her prayer and example;
may we be people of faith, hope, and love,
and may we be always strengthened in our lives
by the promise of everlasting love and joy in heaven.
We make this prayer through Christ our Lord. Amen.

Prayer over the Gifts
Gracious God, accept our gifts of bread and wine,
signs of our faith in you,
small signs of our thanks to you.
We ask that you change us to be more like your Son,
as we receive his body and blood,
the gift of Mary's son,
Jesus Christ, in whose name we pray. Amen.

Invitation to Communion
This is the lamb of God, Jesus Christ, Son of God and Son of Mary.
We are happy to be called to this Eucharist.
Lord I am not ...

Communion Reflection
Nobody thought he'd come like he did:
born like a poor child, in a borrowed house,
the son of a woman seeming no different from any other,
except in her glowing faith and huge generosity.
Long after the kings who envied him have been forgotten,
the name of Jesus, Son of God and Son of Mary,
is remembered in lands not even then heard of.
Long after Mary's own birthplace is forgotten,
or the shape of her face and the age of her death,
we remember that she was a woman who gave to God
her whole life, her whole womanhood,
and because of that 'all generations call her blessed'.

Mary, you remind us of what's best in our human nature –
sympathy, compassion, motherhood, love and care.
You remind us, too, that we are made not just for this life
because as you are now, we one day shall be
through the grace and gift of God.

Concluding Prayer
Give health of mind and body to us, loving God,
through the prayers and love of your Son's mother.
Give us, too, a faith like hers,
a confidence in you like hers,
and a hope like hers,
We make this prayer through Christ Our Lord. Amen.

2. Christmas

Introduction

The streets are crowded now with shoppers and the carols are being sung; there's an air of festivity and of busyness. True, a lot of money is being made and there's a lot of commercialism, but behind it all is a wish for peace on earth and goodwill among people.

Christmas is more than the feast of Christ's birth. It's the feast of the birth of every child of God, in every part of the world. It's the feast of human dignity, that every person born on this earth is loved and cherished by God, and enters the human family where love and care are sought and given.

Christmas can bring out the best in people, roll away clouds of hatred and bitterness and let the song of the angels be heard. Our Christmas trees, the comical mistletoe, the holly and the ivy are all part of the story that God is close to us and that we desire relationships of equality and justice and love.

That's our reflection and our prayer for this Mass at Christmas time. May we all be touched by the love and the simplicity of God as we pray and celebrate this feast together.

Penitential Rite

As we call to mind the goodness of God and the value of each person, we confess that we have not always treated everyone with dignity, nor with the respect that is their due.

Lord Jesus, you are Lord of Life and Prince of Peace:
Lord have mercy.
Lord Jesus, you come with peace and goodwill for all your people:
Christ have mercy.
Lord Jesus, you are raised from death at the right hand of God:
Lord have mercy.

Opening Prayer

God our Father, you are the source of all life,
and have created every man and woman,
in your image and in your love.
We wonder what this means?
Help us to see in the person of everyone we meet

the image of your beauty, love, goodness, and forgiveness,
through Jesus Christ, our Lord. Amen.

First Reading *Isaiah 9:1-7*

> *Christmas is like a light: the brightness of God in the darkness of war and of hatred, of hopelessness and despair. It is the celebration that God is very close to us. That's behind this first reading from Isaiah.*

A reading from the prophet Isaiah.

The people that walked in darkness have seen a great light;
on those who live in a land of great shadow a light has shone.
You have made their gladness greater,
you have made their joy increase.

For there is a child born for us, a son given to us
and dominion is laid on his shoulders;
and this is the name they give him:
Wonder-Counsellor, Mighty-God, Eternal-Father, Prince-of-Peace.
Wide is his dominion in a peace that has no end,
for the throne of David
and for his royal power,
which he establishes and makes secure in justice and integrity.
From this time onwards and forever,
the jealous love of God will do this.

Responsorial Psalm

Psalm 84 A poem about God living among people.
RESPONSE: Glory to God in the highest,
          and peace to God's people on earth.

How lovely is your dwelling place,
Lord, God of hosts. R.

My soul is longing and yearning,
yearning for the courts of the Lord.
My heart and my soul ring out their joy
to God, the living God. R.

Gospel *Luke 2:1-20*

> *We listen to the story – we know it so well – of the birth of Christ, noticing the simple and really human way in which God became man, and the mysteriousness of the choice to be born among the poor.*

A reading from the holy Gospel according to Luke.

Joseph set out from the town of Nazareth in Galilee and travelled up to Judaea, to the town of David called Bethlehem, since he was of David's house and line, in order to be registered together with Mary, his betrothed, who was with child. While they were there the time came for her to have her child, and she gave birth to a son, her first-born. She wrapped him in swaddling clothes, and laid him in a manger because there was no room for them at the inn. In the countryside close by there were shepherds who lived in the fields and took it in turns to watch their flocks during the night. The angel of the Lord appeared to them and the glory of the Lord shone round them. They were terrified, but the angel said, 'Do not be afraid. Listen, I bring you news of great joy, a joy to be shared by the whole people. Today in the town of David a saviour has been born to you; he is Christ the Lord. And here is a sign for you: you will find a baby wrapped in swaddling clothes and lying in a manger.' And suddenly with the angel there was a great throng of the heavenly host, praising God and singing:
'Glory to God in the highest heaven,
and peace to those who enjoy God's favour.'

Prayer of the Faithful
Let's pray now for any intentions and people who come to mind as we remember the birth of Christ.

> We pray that each of us will believe more strongly in the dignity of everyone, and that we'll be more tolerant and less critical in how we think of others and act towards them: Lord hear us.
> *Response: Lord, hear our prayer; Come, Lord Jesus.*
> We pray for peace and for justice in our country and our world; for the forgiveness of God for the way wealthy groups and nations treat those poorer than themselves: Lord hear us. R.
> We remember all our families, living and dead; for those of our family away from home. Bless them, Lord, with joy at Christmas. Lord hear us. R.

Be with us, Lord, as we remember your birth;
we thank you for coming among us as a man,
walking all the ways of our lives,
consolation, comfort and joy in all our days.
Help us to be bearers of your peace and love,
We ask this in your holy name.

Offertory

To the music of Silent Night or any other well-known Christmas carol, some reminders of Christmas might be brought to the altar.

Prayer over the Gifts

God, Father, we bring you bread and wine.
We bring, too, some of the things that remind us of Christmas.
We ask you now to become more and more the center of our lives, so that everything we do reflects the presence of Christ within us.
We ask this in the name of Jesus the Lord. Amen.

Communion Reflection

Why did you come, Lord, the way you did?
Poor, homeless, God-among-us?
Born, not among the leaders and princes whose names are long since forgotten, except for Herod
who wanted to kill you;
born, among the outcasts of society,
within the love of Joseph and Mary.
Why did you come like this?
Maybe the silence of your birth
broken only by the hymn of the angels
the cry of a child and the noise of an animal says it all:
that God is as simple and as complex as a child
and always on the side of the poor.

'Why did you come, Lord, the way you did?'

Concluding Prayer

We pray, gracious God, that each person here may have a happy Christmas, and bring that happiness to family, friends and all we meet.
May the message of Christmas be a sign in our land and in our world, of justice, joy, love, and the friendship of God among us.
We ask this through Christ our Lord. Amen.

3. Ash Wednesday

Introduction

Today ashes are blessed and placed on our foreheads. They are reminders of our sinfulness and of our littleness before God.

These ashes were once the palms used on Palm Sunday. So they are also ashes of hope. We take them to remind us that we are part of the creation of God. We are made by God, as is the earth and its dust, for life. In taking the ashes we are all equal: men and women, young and old, teacher and pupil; we are all equal in the sight of God. We all take the same ashes.

These ashes have no value except in the sight of God. They are nothing but dust. We are nothing without God: in God we live and move and have our being.

Opening Prayer

Father in Heaven,
the light of your truth gives sight to the darkness of sin.
May this season of Lent bring us the blessing
of your forgiveness and the gift of your light.
Grant this through Christ Our Lord.
Amen.

First Reading *Joel 2:13-14*

On Ash Wednesday if time is short (the distribution of ashes takes extra time), consider omitting this first reading.

A reading from the prophet Joel.

Let your hearts be broken, not your garments torn.
Turn to the Lord your God again,
for God is all tenderness and compassion,
slow to anger, rich in graciousness, and ready to relent.

Responsorial Psalm

Psalm 51 A poem of sorrow for sin.
RESPONSE: Have mercy on me, God, in your kindness.

Have mercy on me, God, in your kindness,
in your compassion blot out my offense.

O wash me more and more from my guilt,
and cleanse me from my sin. R.

My offenses truly I know them,
my sin is always before me.
Against you, you alone, have I sinned
what is evil in your sight I have done. R.

Gospel *Mark 1:14–15*

The message of Lent is to change our lives to be more Christian, more unselfish, more compassionate and kind. This is the beginning of the message of Jesus.

A reading from the holy Gospel according to Mark.

After John had been arrested, Jesus went into Galilee. There he proclaimed the Good News from God. 'The time has come', he said 'and the kingdom of God is close at hand. Repent, and believe the Good News.'

Blessing of Ashes

We ask God to bless these ashes,
which we will use as the mark of our redemption.
Reader 1:
Dust to dust and ashes to ashes;
may we remember this day
that we come from God
and will go to God.
Reader 2:
Dust to dust and ashes to ashes;
may we remember this day
that we need God's forgiveness.
Reader 3:
Dust to flowers and ashes to glory:
may we remember this day
that Jesus died and rose from death.

Reflection

What does it mean that we believe
that we came from the dust of the earth?
Not that we were once clay, mud or dust.
That was a way of saying that we came from God.
It was a way of admitting that we, men and women,

are not masters of ourselves.
We did not call ourselves into being.
We came from the breath and life of God.
Warmth breathing life into nothing,
life growing in the safety of the womb,
life bursting forth as flowers from the earth.
What does it mean that we believe
that we came from the dust of the earth?
What does it mean to be alive?
The same answers:
gift of God, joy of God, promise of God.
I am dust;
and flowers grow in dust moistened by the warmth of God.

Prayer over the Gifts
Gracious God, help us to resist the attraction of evil
in the world and in our hearts.
May we give time this Lent to prayer and to good works.
We ask this in the name of Jesus the Lord.
Amen.

Communion Reflection
Who would say that their lives are in ashes?
People who, through no fault of their own,
have bit the dust of the earth:
who live on the dust of the earth and not in a house,
who squat on the bare earth
from whose dust they have eked out
barely enough food to live on,
who cry to the dust of the earth for water,
who cry from the ashes of a broken marriage for help,
or children who suffer in the dust of abuse, of neglect.
Lord, bless them as you have blessed these ashes;
Lord, may we receive them into our lives
as our foreheads received these ashes.
We pray that your living water
may refresh the ashes of our love;
help us to see in each person we meet,
your face, your glory, your delight;
help us to know your cry, your pain, your sorrow
in the faces of all we meet.

Stretch the vision of our eyes to see in everyone your reflection,
of Love, of Joy, of Hope.
Stretch our hearts to love as you do.

Concluding Prayer
God our Father, we have shared the sadness of life
by remembering sin and suffering;
we have shared the joy of life in receiving the Eucharist.
Make us always truly thankful,
through Christ Our Lord.
Amen.

4. Lent 1

Introduction

In this Mass we think of Jesus being led into the wilderness. He was tempted there to go away from the work God wanted him to do. He was tempted by the attraction of power, of wealth, and honor. This was time he spent strengthening himself for his future work: for his preaching, healing, concern for people – work which would lead him to death on the cross. He needed this time to deepen the choices he had already made. He was led into the desert by the Spirit; God wanted him there.

We might think, during the Mass, of the times we have felt we were in the wilderness; when we felt that life was very rough, when we were in conflict with our family, when we were lonely, when we feared failure. Jesus says of himself that he comes looking for us when we feel like that. We ask God for the help to keep doing what we know is right, especially at times when our good intentions may waver.

Penitential Rite

We remember in Lent that our faults can lead us away from God; we also remember that God is all forgiving and all loving. So we ask this forgiveness now for everyone here.

You were led by the Spirit to the desert:
Lord, have mercy.
You were tempted to a life of power and honor and wealth:
Christ have mercy.
You plead with God for us, your people for whom you died:
Lord, have mercy.

May almighty God have mercy on us, forgive us our sins, and bring us to life everlasting. Amen.

Opening Prayer

Lord God,
help us to know what we ought to do in our lives,
to do it with courage and generosity
and always to live in your love.
We ask this through Christ our Lord. Amen.

First Reading *Ezekiel 34:11-16*

This is a story of God looking for us when we are lost. It is a story about God being near us when we feel confused, lonely, misunderstood – any experiences which are like being in a wilderness.

A reading from the prophet Ezekiel.

The Lord says this: I am going to look after my flock myself. As a shepherd keeps all his flock in view when he stands up in the middle of his scattered sheep, so shall I keep my sheep in view. I shall rescue them from wherever they have been scattered during the mist and the darkness. I shall feed them in good pasturage; the high mountains will be their grazing ground. They will rest in good grazing ground; they will browse in rich pastures on the mountains. I myself will pasture my sheep, I myself will show them where to rest: it is the Lord who speaks. I shall look for the lost one, bring back the stray, bandage the wounded and make the weak strong. I shall watch over the fat and healthy. I shall be a true shepherd to them.

Responsorial Psalm

Psalm 27 A poem of trust in God.
RESPONSE: The Lord is my light and my help.

The Lord is my light and my help,
whom shall I fear?
The Lord is the stronghold of my life;
before whom shall I shrink? R.

I am sure I shall see the Lord's goodness
in the land of the living.
Hope in him, hold firm and take heart,
Hope in the Lord! R.

Gospel *Matthew 3:1-10*

In the wilderness Jesus was tempted to depart from what he knew was his life's mission. He knew confusion, questioning, and also knew that God was with him in the tough times of his own life.

A reading from the holy Gospel according to Matthew.

Jesus was led by the Spirit out into the wilderness to be tempted by the devil. He fasted for forty days and forty nights, after which he was very hungry, and the tempter came and said to him, 'If you are the Son of God, tell these stones to turn into loaves.' But he replied, 'Scripture says: A person does not live on bread alone, but on every

word that comes from the mouth of God.' The devil then took him to
the holy city and made him stand on the parapet of the Temple. 'If
you are the Son of God', he said, 'throw yourself down, for Scripture
says: He will put you in his angels' charge, and they will support you
on their hands in case you hurt your foot against a stone.' Jesus said to
him, 'Scripture also says: You must not put the Lord your God to the
test.' Next, taking him to a very high mountain, the devil showed him
all the kingdoms of the world and their splendour. 'I will give you all
these,' he said, 'if you fall at my feet and worship me.' Then Jesus replied, 'Be off, Satan! For scripture says: You must worship the Lord
your God, and serve him alone.' Then the devil left him, and angels
appeared and looked after him.

Prayer of the Faithful

We make our intentions and prayers to God:

> We ask that we ourselves always know the care of God in the hard
> times of our lives; Lord, hear us.
> For people we know who are in any sort of trouble, particularly
> members of our own families; Lord, hear us.
> For young people who are lost, lonely, and confused, we pray they
> find friendship and a sense of direction in their lives; Lord, hear us.
> We pray that our faith may grow strong, and that our doubts and
> difficulties may not take us away from God; Lord, hear us.
> For all who have died, people we know and those of our family,
> and all who die unmourned, unloved and unremembered; Lord,
> hear us.

God our Father, hear our prayers which we make in faith, in hope and
in love, through Jesus Christ our Lord. Amen.

Prayer over the Gifts

Gracious God, accept our gifts of bread and wine.
As we receive from this table the Eucharist of your Son,
help us always to look to you for love, meaning and hope in our lives.
We ask this through Christ our Lord.
Amen.

Communion Reflection

What does it mean to be led into the wilderness?
To find yourself without bearings,
without direction,
without food, drink, company?

For many the wilderness is to be without direction.
Not knowing how to find love, meaning, joy in life.
Losing faith, hope, friends, commitment.
This seems to be part of life.
In the wilderness Jesus was tempted
to lose direction and to change his plans.
Can you allow yourself to find refreshment,
faith, self-confidence
when you feel in the wilderness of aloneness
or of failure or confusion?
In your desert wilderness you will know God
who comes looking for you then.
If you trust and hope you will know that you are not lost,
for God will come to find you.

Concluding Prayer
God our Father,
you have given us the food of life at this table.
Help us always to know your friendship in our lives.
In times of sorrow, be our strength
and in times of joy, be our companion.
We ask this through Christ our Lord.
Amen.

5. Lent 2

Introduction

Our Mass today emphasizes the theme of water. Jesus says in the gospel that what he wants to give us is the living water, a fountain or wellspring of life inside us, which is his love.

We'll start our Mass by pouring out a bowl of water. Look at it and think that water is something we connect with life and with growth: we are surrounded by the protection of water in the womb and we need it to grow. It is something we connect with cleansing and with baptism. We are forgiven in the waters which cleanse us and called to follow Jesus in the water of baptism. Themes of forgiveness, cleansing, renewal, refreshment, and growth are themes for Masses in Lent.

We begin our Mass with a prayer of blessing on this bowl of water.

Penitential Rite

This water comes from the earth,
a wellspring of God's creation.
Or it comes from the clouds and the sky,
made by the living word of God.
We ask you, Lord, to bless this water.
May it be for us a sign of our baptism,
and may it open our hearts and minds to the love of God.
May it also be a sign of forgiveness;
we pour our sins into this water,
and know we are putting them into the forgiving love of Christ.
Grant this through Christ our Lord. Amen.

After the blessing of the water, each person comes and makes the sign of the cross on his or her forehead; or the priest can do so; or the bowls can be passed around and each person can make the sign of the cross on the next person's forehead. During this, a song should be sung or some music played. After the signing of the cross, the priest says:

May almighty God have mercy on us, forgive us our sins, and bring us to life everlasting. Amen.

Opening Prayer

Gracious God, your love for us is new and strong every day of our lives.

Help us to receive this love into our lives, as the earth receives water.
May your love grow within us,
so that our lives mirror the love you have for your people.
We make this prayer through Christ Our Lord. Amen.

First Reading *Isaiah 55:1-3*
> *In this reading we are invited to welcome God's love into our lives.
> This is an invitation to people who are tired and weary to come to the
> refreshment of water; an invitation to people looking for meaning and
> hope in their lives to receive it from God.*

A reading from the prophet Isaiah.

Oh, come to the water, all you who are thirsty;
though you have no money, come!
Buy corn without money, and eat,
and at no cost, wine and milk.
Why spend money on what is not bread,
your wages on what fails to satisfy?
Listen, listen to me,
and you will have good things to eat and rich food to enjoy.
Pay attention, come to me, listen and your soul will live.

Responsorial Psalm
Psalm 95 A poem of joy in God.
RESPONSE: Let us give thanks to God all the days of our life.

Come, sing out your joy to the Lord,
greet the rock who saves us.
Let us come before him, giving thanks,
with songs let us greet the Lord. R.

Come in, let us bow and bend low;
let us kneel before the God who made us
for he is our God and we the people who belong to his pasture,
the flock that is led by his hand. R.

Gospel *John 4:7–10*
> *A lady who is weary of an empty life comes to Jesus, and is offered the
> friendship of Jesus. This is offered also to us. It is something which will
> never end. It is a hope and a meaning in our lives which is fuller than
> any other.*

A reading from the holy Gospel according to John.

When a Samaritan woman came to the well where Jesus was, Jesus said to her, 'Give me a drink.' His disciples had gone into the town to buy food. The Samaritan woman said, 'What? You are a Jew, and you ask me, a Samaritan, for a drink?' Jews in fact do not associate with Samaritans. Jesus replied, 'If only you knew what God is offering and who it is that is saying to you: 'Give me a drink,' you would have been the one to ask, and he would have given you living water. Whoever drinks this water will get thirsty again; but anyone who drinks the water that I shall give, will never be thirsty again. The water that I shall give will turn into a spring inside you, welling up to eternal life.'

Prayer of the Faithful
As we join together for this Mass, let us pray for each other's intentions:

For all our families: parents, brothers, and sisters, may God bless them, especially any who are in trouble at the moment. Lord, hear us.

For those who are sick, friends or family particularly, may God give them strength in their illness and loved ones to care for them. Lord, hear us.

For those who work for young people, people trying to create employment, and those who work with young people who are in any sort of trouble; may God help them in their work. Lord, hear us.

For those who have died, especially people who are close to us, and those who have died young, as well as those who die in accidents and violence. Lord, hear us.

Let us pray:
God our Father, hear our prayers which we make to you in faith, in hope and in love, through Jesus Christ our Lord. Amen.

Prayer over the Gifts
We give you bread and wine
that they may become the life of your Son, Jesus Christ.
We give you ourselves
that we may be filled with the life of Jesus,
the life of love, justice, and forgiveness.
We ask this in the name of Jesus the Lord. Amen.

Communion Reflection
Who is she?
Who is the woman at the well?

She is the confused person, young or old,
looking for meaning in life,
and wondering where to find it.

Who is the woman at the well?
She is the lonely person, young, middle-aged, old,
who is looking for love,
who has looked for it in the wrong places
or tasted only its pleasures but not its joys.

Who is the woman at the well?
You and me when we fail,
when we hate ourselves,
when we want freedom from our guilt,
when we want light not darkness in our lives,
when we want to know that love can last,
that compassion can heal,
that life is forever.

The truth that Jesus is God and he is a friend,
the truth that love is a mystery and is around us,
the truth that God's love reaches deeply into us
and is a wellspring for ever,
This is the promise of Jesus,
'I will give you living water.'
If only we ask!

Concluding Prayer
God our Father,
in baptism you promised you would always be with us.
We ask you now to help us in everything in our lives,
particularly in study, work, friendship and family.
We make this prayer through Christ our Lord. Amen.

6. Holy Week

Introduction
At this time of year we think of the death of Jesus. His death was the result of the courage of his convictions. He had lived his life with a message of compassion, of equality, of love for the poor, at times criticizing the powerful for lording it over the weak. He died at the hands of injustice; everyone connected with his death was in some way covering his own skin. Jesus is an example, like many after him, of the battle of good and evil. And of the battle of love and of selfishness. This battle is fought inside ourselves too, as we live our lives between the attraction of the good and the pull of evil. At the beginning of our Mass, we light our candles around the cross and pray that good may overcome evil in our world, that justice may overcome injustice in our land, and that love may overcome selfishness in our own lives.

Penitential Rite
As we prepare to celebrate the Mass, we recall the forgiveness of God in Jesus on the Cross and ask for that forgiveness in our lives.
> You forgave everyone from the Cross of your pain and death:
> Lord, have mercy.
> You promised eternal life to all your people from the Cross:
> Christ, have mercy.
> You are the One who has overcome the evil of death and of sin:
> Lord, have mercy.
> May almighty God have mercy on us, forgive us our sins,
> and bring us to life everlasting. Amen.

Opening Prayer
Gracious God,
in the death of Jesus your Son,
you have given a sure sign of your love in the world.
Through his death and resurrection, good has overcome evil.
May we, in our lives, be signs of the victory of good over evil,
peace over war, love over selfishness.
Grant this through Christ our Lord. Amen.

First Reading *Philippians 2:6–11*
> *This is a hymn of praise to Christ the Lord who suffered at the hands of his people, and who is now at the right hand of God.*

A reading from the letter of Paul to the Philippians.

Jesus' state was divine, yet he did not cling to his equality with God; but emptied himself to assume the condition of a slave, and became as all people are; and being as we all are, he was humbler yet, even to accepting death, death on a cross. But God raised him high and gave him the name which is above all other names, so that all beings in heaven, on earth, or in the underworld, should bend the knee at the name of Jesus, and that every tongue should acclaim Jesus Christ as Lord, to the glory of God the Father.

Responsorial Psalm *Psalm 22*
RESPONSE: My God, why have you deserted me?

My God, my God why have you deserted me?
How far from saving me, the words I groan!
I call all day, my God, but you never answer,
all night long I call and cannot rest. R.

Here am I, now more worm than man,
the scorn of mankind, jest of the people,
all who see me jeer at me,
they toss their heads and sneer. R.

'If God is his friend, let him rescue him!'.
But God has not despised or disdained the poor man in his poverty,
has not hidden his face from him,
but has answered when he called him. R.

Gospel *Luke 23: 44–48*
> *This is the account of the death of Jesus, of the sadness of those who watched it, even of his friends who watched from a distance. The death of Jesus was a lonely death.*

A reading from the holy Gospel according to Luke.

It was now about the sixth hour and, with the sun eclipsed, a darkness came over the whole land until the ninth hour. The veil of the Temple was torn right down the middle; and when Jesus had cried out in a loud voice, he said, 'Father, into your hands I commit my spirit.' With these words he breathed his last. When the centurion saw what had taken place, he praised God and said, 'This was a great and good man.' And when all the people who had gathered for the spectacle saw what had happened, they went home beating their breasts. All his friends stood at a distance; so also did the women who had accompanied him from Galilee, and they saw all this happen.

Prayer of the Faithful

In our prayers at this Mass we remember people who suffer in the cause of goodness and of right, and who live lives of love and self-lessness:

> We pray for our families, that we may be grateful for the love and the thoughtfulness we show to each other; in this way love is stronger than selfishness; Lord, hear us.
>
> We pray for men and women who suffer in the cause of what is right and in obedience to their convictions; in this way truth overcomes a false way of life; Lord, hear us.
>
> We pray for people in all parts of the world who are suffering in the cause of equality and of human rights; in this way justice overcomes injustice and good is stronger than evil; Lord, hear us.
>
> We pray for people working for peace based on justice, in our own country and in all parts of the world; in this way love overcomes violence and good is stronger than evil; Lord, hear us.

Prayer over the Gifts

Lord, as we offer these gifts of bread and wine,
help us to serve you in prayer and good works.
By our sharing in the Mass during these weeks
may we prepare well to celebrate
the death and resurrection of Jesus Christ our Saviour.
We ask this through Christ our Lord. Amen.

Invitation to Communion

We receive now the bread of life, the body of Christ broken in suffering for our sins. It is the bread that invites us to work with him for his suffering people. We are happy to be called to this Eucharist.
Lord, I am not worthy to receive you,
but only say the word and I shall be healed.

Communion Reflection

There is too much of Pilate in us to be hard on him.
Worldly people might even say
Pilate did not do too badly to hold out so long.
Yet the very familiarity of his behavior,
the sneaking sympathy it engages,
together with its appalling consequences,

is precisely what makes his story so disturbing.
In private, at work, in public office,
the conflict between conviction
and wanting to save one's own skin
runs through life like a dark thread.
The pressures may not be so dramatic,
perhaps only the desire not to seem troublesome,
or too noticeable, or eccentric.
In the everyday world it is easier to be Pilate
than the honest juror.
But for the Christian believer
the figure of Pilate is a perpetually haunting presence,
an uncomfortable reminder
that as well as a clear head and a warm heart,
the Christian needs a strong backbone.

John Harriot

Concluding Prayer
Gracious God,
help us in any suffering or sorrow we have.
Help us to know that you care
and feed us with the bread of life.
Give us also a willingness to help others in need.
We ask this through Christ our Lord. Amen.

7. The Cross

Introduction
The cross is the sign that all Christians recognize. It's a reminder of God's love breaking through human violence; it's a sign that no greater love can exist than to suffer with others; it's the sign of the completeness of God's care, for it went beyond death. It's a symbol of hope and of courage, the one thing to which we can all raise our eyes and be consoled, comforted, and challenged. It has done this for centuries because of the man who made it famous. It's how we welcome our children into life and send our dying people forward to eternity, with the sign of the cross. It's a sign of hope, not death; the man on it is a king; rather than a picture of degradation, it is a throne. We allow ourselves to look at this sign during Mass today, to be touched by it. Let it move us to be loving, to yearn for justice, to ask forgiveness for our sins. It is the great sign of reconciliation, of people reaching out to people, from one corner of the world to another. The Mass is the prayer of the Man of the Cross, of Jesus, who wants to be remembered through bread and wine, and the sign of the cross.

Penitential Rite
We come to God confident of forgiveness. On the cross Jesus forgave those who had harmed him. We have all harmed him by hurting others. We look on the cross and ask for forgiveness.
Father, forgive them for they do not know what they are doing:
Lord have mercy.
Today you will be with me in Paradise:
Christ have mercy.
Father, into your hands I commend my spirit:
Lord have mercy.

Opening Prayer
God, our Father, we rejoice in the victory of Jesus over death.
Your power is stronger than evil, because love is the strongest power of all.
We know we need the help of Christ who suffered for us.
We pray for all those who need his friendship, and ask for the gift of trust in your power to bring good out of evil, as you raised him to new life from death.
We ask this through Christ our Lord. Amen.

First Reading *Philippians 2:5–11*

The Cross is raised up like a bright light over the whole world, to show that goodness is powerful and that love is strong. It is the sign of the glory of Christ, the friend wounded for sin. That's behind this prayer of St Paul:

A reading from the letter of Paul to the Philippians.

In your minds you must be the same as Christ Jesus:
His state was divine,
yet he did not cling to his equality with God
but emptied himself to assume the condition of a slave,
and become as we are;
and being as we are, he was humbler yet,
even accepting death, death on a cross.
But God raised him high
and gave him the name
which is above all other names so that all beings
in the heavens, on earth and in the underworld,
should bend the knee at the name of Jesus
and that every tongue should acclaim Jesus Christ as Lord,
to the glory of God the Father.

Responsorial Psalm
Psalm 22 This psalm was prayed by Jesus on the Cross.
RESPONSE: Lord, we rejoice in your victory over death.

My God, my God, why have you forsaken me?
You are far from my plea and the cry of my distress.
O my God, I call by day and you give me no reply;
I call by night and I find no peace. R.

I can count every one of my bones.
These people stare at me and gloat;
they divide my clothing among them.
They cast lots for my robe. R.

And my soul shall live for him, my children serve him.
They shall tell of the Lord to generations yet to come,
declare his faithfulness to peoples yet unborn:
'These things the Lord has done.' R.

Gospel *Luke 23:33-34, 39-46*

Notice the forgiveness of Jesus: the care, concern and compassion he has from the cross. He still suffers where we suffer, and calls us in our own way to heal the suffering of people wherever we can.

A reading from the holy Gospel according to Luke.

When they reached the place called The Skull, they crucified him there and the two criminals also, one on the right, the other on the left. Jesus said, 'Father, forgive them; they do not know what they are do-ing.' Then they cast lots to share out his clothing.

One of the criminals hanging there abused him, 'Are you not the Christ?' he said. 'Save yourself and us as well.' But the other spoke up and rebuked him. 'Have you no fear of God at all?' he said. 'You got the same sentence as he did, but in our case we deserved it: we are pay-ing for what we did. But this man has done nothing wrong. 'Jesus,' he said, 'remember me when you come into your kingdom.' 'Indeed, I promise you,' he replied. 'today you will be with me in paradise.'

It was now about the sixth hour and, with the sun eclipsed, a darkness came over the whole land until the ninth hour. The veil of the Temple was torn right down the middle; and when Jesus had cried out in a loud voice, he said, 'Father into your hands I commit my spirit.' With these words he breathed his last.

Prayer of the Faithful
We pray especially at this Mass for the people who need our prayers and our help in their sufferings.

For people who are sick, young people who are in any way disabled or handicapped, for children who are born with any disease, and for those parents, family, nurses, doctors who look after them:
Response: Lord you have shared our human suffering, hear our prayer.
For men and women everywhere who suffer through injustice and the greed of others; through violence and war; for those who have little food and inadequate housing. Be with them in their suffering: Lord hear us. R.
Help us to be sensitive to the sufferings of others, to see, hear, and feel your pain in the pain of your people, especially those who are lonely: Lord hear us. R.
Lord God, you have shown us hope and courage
in the mystery of the Cross.
We want to help others in their suffering
and we ourselves want to grow through our pain.

Help us to see Jesus as a companion and friend
especially when we are troubled.
We ask this in the name of Jesus the Lord. Amen.

Prayer over the Gifts
Lord God, we offer our gifts of bread and wine,
reminders to us of the death and resurrection of Jesus.
Help us, through prayer,
to be able to recognize the cross in the lives of others,
and be sensitive instruments of your peace and love.
We ask this in the name of Jesus the Lord. Amen.

Communion Reflection
The cross of Christ reaches from earth to heaven,
a link between our suffering and God's love.
We make crosses for each other, and people die and suffer, in famine,
loneliness and neglect,
because we fail to see, hear, and feel their needs.
There's abuse of the poor and of children,
the confusion of the adolescent,
the pain of the old and lonely.
The cross is a cry of triumph and of God's presence,
a challenge to believe that nothing of evil will last,
but that courage and friendship can spread justice and peace.
Can we be the link between human suffering and God's love?

Concluding Prayer
Bless each person here, Father, before we go.
As we gather in the name of Jesus
may we be strengthened to live in his name too.
We ask this through Christ our Lord. Amen.

8. Easter 1

Introduction

We've put flowers around the room for this Mass because it's a Mass about Easter. A key word for Easter is joy. Jesus has said that he came so that we would have joy to the full.

It's worth just asking what sort of joy this is. The joy of succeeding in an exam? The joy of being in love? The joy of a good football game? There are many sorts of joy in our lives: the joy of Jesus at Easter is the lasting joy. After pain, violence, and death he knows now he has overcome it all.

There is no darkness in life which his joy cannot touch. He gives hope in every situation of life: in rejection, in bereavement, in sickness, failure, and in death itself.

Our Mass is a prayer to have some of this joy and to know that it lasts forever, in this life and in the next.

Penitential Rite

Let us ask God's forgiveness for times when we have shown the selfish, unhappy side of ourselves to others, when it could have been otherwise: Lord Jesus you said, 'I have come that you may have joy and have it to the full.'
I confess ...

Opening Prayer

Almighty God,
may the risen power and love of Jesus Christ
be felt in our lives,
our families, our schools, and our parishes.
May we know it in our country and in our world.
We ask this through Christ our Lord. Amen.

First Reading *Acts 2:22-28*

> *This is a sermon from Peter after the resurrection: he quotes a poem from the bible which expresses the joy of the heart, mind and body at the sight of God. This was the apostles' joy after the first Easter.*

A reading from the Acts of the Apostles.

Then Peter stood up with the Eleven and addressed the crowd in a

loud voice: Men of Israel, listen to what I am going to say: Jesus the
Nazarene was a man commended to you by God, by the miracles and
portents and signs that God worked through him when he was among
you, as you all know. You killed him, but God raised him to life, for it
was impossible for him to be held in the power of death, as David says
of him:

I saw the Lord before me always,
for with him at my right hand nothing can shake me.
So my heart was glad, and my tongue cried out with joy;
my body, too, will rest in the hope
that you will not abandon my soul to Hades,
nor allow your Holy One to know corruption.
You have made known the way of life to me,
you will fill me with joy through your presence.

Responsorial Psalm
Psalm 46 A poem of triumph of God over evil.
RESPONSE: Lord, you are our victory over evil.

God is our shelter, our strength,
ever ready to help in time of trouble,
so we shall not be afraid when the earth gives way,
when mountains tumble into the depths of the sea,
and its waters roar and seethe. R.

Come, think of the marvels of the Lord,
the astounding things he has done in the world;
all over the world he puts an end to wars,
he breaks the bow, he snaps the spear.
'Pause a while and know that I am God,
exalted among the nations, exalted over the earth. R.

Gospel *Luke 24:36-43*
   The apostles are frightened first at the appearance of Jesus, but even-
   tually they 'are filled with joy'.
A reading from the holy Gospel according to Luke.

They were still talking about all this when he himself stood among
them and said to them, 'Peace be with you!' In a state of alarm and
fright, they thought they were seeing a ghost. But he said, 'Why are
you so agitated, and why are these doubts rising in your hearts? Look
at my hands and feet; yes, it is I indeed. Touch me and see for yourselves; a ghost has no flesh and bones as you can see I have.' And as he

said this he showed them his hands and his feet. Their joy was so great that they still could not believe it, and they stood there dumbfounded; so he said to them, 'Have you anything here to eat?' And they offered him a piece of grilled fish, which he ate before their eyes.

Prayer of the Faithful
Jesus prayed for peace after his resurrection, and that his followers would be people of unity and of forgiveness. Let's make our intentions now in his name:

Give us joy, Lord, in knowing that you are always with us, a companion in good times and bad, comfort in our losses; Lord, hear us.

Give peace to troubled parts of the world, especially in our own country; Lord, hear us.

Give hope to people who are down and troubled, especially young people who fear failure and rejection in their lives; Lord, hear us.

Give eternal joy to all who have died, especially people in our families and others we know; Lord, hear us.

We pray for the sick, the forgotten, the handicapped, the lonely: give them the consolation of your risen power; Lord, hear us.

Let us pray:
God, Creator of everything we love, hear our prayer which we make in trust in you. Give us joy and freedom in your risen Son, Jesus Christ our Lord. Amen.

Prayer over the Gifts
May these gifts we offer
be signs of our love for you, Almighty God,
and for each other.
As you change them into the body and blood of Jesus,
change us too that we become people of joy and hope.
Grant this through Christ our Lord. Amen.

Communion Reflection
We ran then, John and I, uphill,
and I couldn't keep up with his young lungs.
Sure enough, the stone was rolled back.
John peered in but was staying outside.
I went right in.
No body!
I saw the cloths,
and the cloth for the face was over on its own.

My mind was all confused.
Now, who would take the body
and go to the trouble of taking off the winding cloths?
It was very valuable linen.
John had come in. He was very quiet.
He whispered something. I did not quite catch it at first.
'He is risen! Resurrection, remember!'
I nearly passed out with shock.
'Remember Lazarus ... the day in Nain, remember that girl of Jairus.'
I remembered alright.
Remembered that morning on the lake with the fish.
Remembered waking up that day on the mountain.
Remembered a hundred stunning moments.
How could we have forgotten?
It was we who were in the tomb;
we who were in darkness.
And it wasn't a stone in front of the tomb,
but a deep, dark cloud of self pity.
There is no such thing as a tomb unless it is in yourself.
There is never an end to hope.
And in Jesus there is no such thing as death as we used to know it.

Silvester O'Flynn, OFM Cap.

Concluding Prayer
Bless us, gracious God,
as we leave the table and the Eucharist of your risen Son.
May we bring with us the hope, peace, and joy
which we find in the resurrection of Jesus
who is Lord, today and forever. Amen.

9. Easter 2

Introduction

In the life of Jesus, after his resurrection, you see him bringing peace, joy, consolation to many different people. When people meet him they know once again that he is alive, and they seem to want to share this good news.

In the Mass today, we try to hear this good news about Jesus: that death and violence and injustice didn't kill him, but that he does his work now in a different way. We are part of his risen life, and the way he works in the world today is through us. Whenever we look after the lonely or the down and out, try to make life's conditions better for people who are in any way deprived, then we are sharing in the work of the resurrection.

The call of the resurrection to is to spread faith and justice in our world: faith in Jesus as the word and love of God, and the justice of God, seen in the words and life of Jesus, the risen Lord.

Penitential Rite

Jesus sends his apostles as the Father sent him: to bring reconciliation and justice into the world. Let us ask his forgiveness for times when we have failed to be people of reconciliation and of justice when it could have been otherwise.

> Lord Jesus, you said, 'I have come that you may have joy and have it to the full':
> Lord, have mercy.
> Lord Jesus, you said to your apostles, 'I leave you peace, my peace I give you':
> Christ, have mercy.
> Lord Jesus, you are our risen brother, pleading for us at the right hand of the Father:
> Lord, have mercy.

May almighty God have mercy on us, forgive us our sins, and bring us to life everlasting. Amen.

Opening Prayer

Almighty God,
may the risen power and love of Jesus Christ
be felt in our lives, our families, our schools, and our parishes.

May we know it in our country and in our world.
We ask this through Christ our Lord. Amen.

First Reading *Ephesians 2:17-22*

Because of the victory of Jesus over death, we are all united into one community in him. God lives in each of us: that's why we feel the call to share a life of justice and of reconciliation.

A reading from the letter of Paul to the Ephesians.

Jesus came to bring the good news of peace, peace to you who were far away and peace to those who were near at hand. Through him, both of us have, in the one Spirit, our way to come to the Father. So you are no longer aliens or foreign visitors: you are citizens like all the saints and part of God's household. You are part of a building that has the apostles and the prophets for its foundation, and Christ Jesus himself for its main cornerstone. As every structure is aligned on him, all grow into one body, holy temple in the Lord; and you, too, in him, are being built into a house where God lives in the Spirit.

Responsorial Psalm

Psalm 119 A poem about Jesus being the foundation of our lives.
RESPONSE: Lord, we are glad because of your resurrection from the dead.

Give thanks to the Lord, for he is good,
his love is everlasting.
Let all God's people say it,
His love is everlasting. R.

The stone which the builders rejected
has become the corner stone.
This is the Lord's own work,
a marvel in our eyes. R.

Gospel *Mark 16:14-20*

The resurrection of Jesus is accompanied by signs of healing and of new life and faith. The risen power of the Lord today brings healing to our society.

A reading from the holy Gospel according to Mark.

Lastly he showed himself to the Eleven themselves while they were at table ... He said to them, 'Go out into the whole world; proclaim the good News to all creation ... These are the signs which will be associated with believers: in my name they will cast out devils; they will have the gift of tongues; they will pick up snakes in their hands and be unharmed should they drink deadly poison; they will lay their hands upon the sick who will recover.' And so the Lord Jesus, after he had spoken to them, was taken up into heaven: there at the right hand of God he took his place, while they, going out, preached everywhere, the Lord working with them and confirming the word by the signs that accompanied it.

Prayer of the Faithful

Jesus prayed for peace after his resurrection, and he prayed that his followers would be people of unity and of forgiveness. Let's make our intentions now in his name:

> Give us joy, Lord, in knowing that you are always with us, a companion in good times and bad, comfort in our losses; Lord, hear us.
> Give peace to troubled parts of the world, especially in our own country; Lord, hear us.
> Give hope to people who are down and troubled, especially young people who fear failure and rejection in their lives; Lord, hear us.
> Give eternal joy to all who have died, especially people in our families and others we know; Lord, hear us.
> We pray for the sick, the forgotten, the handicapped, the lonely: give them the consolation of your risen power. Lord, hear us.

Let us pray:
God, Creator of everything we love,
hear our prayer which we make in trust.
Give us joy and freedom in your risen Son,
Jesus Christ our Lord. Amen.

Prayer over the Gifts

May these gifts we offer
be signs of our love for you, Lord God, and for each other.
As you change them into the body and blood of Jesus,
change us, too, that we become people of joy and hope.
Grant this through Christ our Lord. Amen.

Communion Reflection

Where is the Lord?
Gone away? His work finished?
How are his followers?

Separating? Their hopes finished?
He is with God.
He is raised to God,
not just raised by God or in God,
but brought on high to God.
He lives now in the place where he was before time began:
with the Father.
He lives with God and he is found in his people;
to be found among people is to be found with God.
Where do we find the One who is with God?
In Galilee, on the road to Emmaus, at the seaside,
among people.
Lord, help me to notice you,
follow you, enjoy you, embrace you, in your people.
Risen Lord, raise your people!

Concluding Prayer
Bless us, loving God,
as we leave the table and the Eucharist of your risen Son.
May we bring with us the hope, peace, and joy
which we find in the resurrection of Jesus who is Lord,
today and forever. Amen.

10. Beginning the School Year

Introduction

This is the Mass to begin our school year. In it we pray for each other, and for the whole school. We'll be asking God's help with our study, our friendships, our sports, our hobbies, and with everything that is part of our school life.

We might feel anxious about the coming year, or we might feel very confident and glad to start again. No matter what, we put ourselves before God to ask for help in the coming year.

And we start by expressing our gratitude. We have many things to be grateful for. Pause for a moment now and think of something you are thankful for just now ... And then think of what else in your life you want to say thanks for: sports, or art, or writing, or dancing, or whatever. Be thankful for your health, your intelligence, your body, your mind. Be grateful for your friends, for your teachers, for being part of this school. Though there are always things we don't like about school, there is much we would miss if we weren't here.

Penitential Rite

As we begin our Mass, we ask God's forgiveness for our faults and failings, for our sinfulness and particularly for ways in which we needlessly hurt each other.

You have come to bring us the life of love:
Lord, have mercy. R.
You have come to bring us the light of truth:
Christ, have mercy. R.
You plead for us at the right hand of God our Father:
Lord, have mercy. R.

Opening Prayer

Help us, God our Father, at the beginning of our school year.
Help us in our work and in our friendships.
We ask this through Christ our Lord.
Amen.

First Reading *Ephesians 3:14-21*

We look ahead to another year. Our first reading is a prayer of St.

Paul for people he taught. He prays that we might grow strong in different areas of our lives. We make this prayer our own for today.

A reading from the letter of Paul to the Ephesians.

This then is what I pray, kneeling before the Father: In the abundance of his glory may he, through his Spirit, enable your inner selves to grow strong, so that Christ may live in your hearts through faith, and then, planted in love and built on love, with all God's holy people you will have the strength to grasp the breadth and the length, the height and the depth; so that, knowing the love of Christ which is beyond all knowledge, you may be filled with the utter fullness of God. Glory be to him whose power, working in us, can do infinitely more than we can ask or imagine; glory be to him in the Church and in Christ Jesus for ever and ever. Amen.

Responsorial Psalm
Psalm 36. A prayer of trust for the coming year.
RESPONSE: Be our help in the days to come.

If you trust in the Lord and do good,
then you will live in the land and be secure.
If you find your delight in the Lord,
he will grant your heart's desire. R.

Commit your life to the Lord,
trust in him and he will act,
so that your justice beaks forth like the light,
and your cause like the noonday sun. R.

Gospel *Mark 4:35-41*
When we look to another year, we don't know what's in store; will it be a happy year, or a difficult one? The gospel is a story of trusting in the presence of Jesus. As he was present in the apostles' rough times, so he is present always with us.

A reading from the holy Gospel according to Mark.

With the coming of evening that same day, he said to them, 'Let us cross over to the other side.' And leaving the crowd behind they took him, just as he was, in the boat; and there were other boats with him. Then it began to blow a great gale and the waves were breaking into the boat so that it was almost swamped. But he was in the stern, his head on the cushion, asleep. They woke him, and said to him, 'Master, do you not care? We are lost!' And he woke up, and rebuked the wind and said to the sea, 'Quiet now! Be calm!' And the wind dropped, and there followed a great calm. Then he said to them, 'Why are you so frightened? Have you still no faith?' They were overcome with awe and said to one another, 'Who can this be? Even the wind and the sea obey him.'

Prayer of the Faithful

Let us make our prayers to God, as we pray at the beginning of our school year:

Look after us, Lord, during this coming year; help us live in this school as a Chrisitan community. Lord, hear us.

We pray for all who work in our school, for teachers and all its staff; bless them and their families. Lord, hear us.

We pray for all past pupils, for those who left last year; we remember especially those who are sick, unemployed, or in any sort of trouble. Lord, hear us.

For any of our former students who have died: Lord have mercy on them and welcome them home to heaven. Lord, hear us.

We pray for people who are new in our school, pupils and teachers; may they be happy here and find friends. Lord, hear us.

Let us pray:

Help us, gracious God, to use well the talents you have given us. Help us bring them to our studies so that we work to the best of our ability. May all in this school feel valued for who we are in your sight. May all we do and learn be in your service, and in the service of love, both now and in the future. We ask this in the name of Jesus our Lord. Amen.

Prayer over the Gifts

Almighty God, accept our gifts and see the goodness of your people who offer them to you. Free us from the influence of evil in our lives by the power of Jesus who is Lord for ever and ever. Amen.

Communion Reflection

What will this year bring?
We do not know;
It will likely bring its usual times of work and play,
experiences of success and failure,
all the things that are part of school life.
It is a new beginning;

the planting of a seed that will grow for a year,
the seed of fruit that will blossom in times to come.
It offers new hope;
hope for good work, for successful results,
for friendship, for fun, for learning.
In this coming year, may there be learning, prayer and fun.
May there be hard work, faith and friendship.
May no one in this school be lonely;
may no one be left out in class;
may no one suffer because of how others here treat them.
As we begin this year in hope, in prayer and in friendship,
may God begin it with us, be with us during it,
and successfully bring it to its conclusion.

Concluding Prayer
May we who have received the love of God at this Mass, spread this love wherever we are; we ask that in this coming year we share the love, kindness, and compassion of God in our school. We make this prayer through Christ our Lord. Amen.

11. Exam Time

Introduction

Exam times are times when we especially feel the need to pray. We can't really expect God to make up for any lack of work, nor to give magic answers. But it is an important time, when we need the calm and the peace that can come from confidence in our friendship with Christ. The knowledge of his care and friendship can calm our anxieties.

Exams can also bring out the worst in a person. Our relationship with Christ helps us cope with any anxieties, competitiveness, or narrow judgments of people. We are human beings long before we take our exams and our way of viewing each other is not on performance in exams but as children of God, brothers and sisters one to another. We'll pray over that at our Mass, as well as praying for the reward of our efforts.

Penitential Rite

We ask God's forgiveness for ways in which we have misused our talents or failed to use them to the good. We ask forgiveness for our laziness, and for the ways we judge each other on the results of our studies, either jealousy of those more successful or looking down on those who fail.

Lord Jesus, you are a friend of sinners and our hope when we feel anxious:
Lord have mercy.
Lord Jesus, you are the brother and friend to all of us:
Christ have mercy.
Lord Jesus, you plead for us at the right hand of the Father:
Lord have mercy.

Opening Prayer

Gracious God, some of us are anxious, worried, or tense about exams; we ask you for your gifts of peace and calm during this time. Help us to do our best so that we can reap the rewards of our study. Help us also to be true friends and a support to others. We give you the gift of our work so that we can use our talents now and in the future in your service.
We ask this through Christ our Lord. Amen.

First Reading *1 Peter 1:3-9*
> *This reading from St. Peter describes our relationship with God: we are loved by God, sometimes tested. Exam time can test our faith as well as our confidence in ourselves.*

A reading from the first letter of Peter.

Blessed be God the Father of our Lord Jesus Christ, who in his great mercy has given us a new birth by raising Jesus Christ from the dead, so that we have a sure hope and the promise of an inheritance that can never be spoiled and never fade away, because it is being kept for you in the heavens. Through your faith, God's power will guard you until the salvation which has been prepared is revealed at the end of time. This is a cause of great joy for you, even though you may for a short time have to bear being plagued by all sorts of trials; so that, when Jesus Christ is revealed, your faith will have been tested and proved like gold – only it is more precious than gold, which is corruptible even though it bears testing by fire – and then you will have praise and glory and honor. You did not see him, yet you love him; and still without seeing him, you are already filled with a joy so glorious that it cannot be described, because you believe; and you are sure of the end to which your faith looks forward, that is, the salvation of your souls.

Responsorial Psalm
Psalm 86 A prayer of trust at a time of need.
RESPONSE: God guides me along the right path.

Lord, listen to my prayer,
turn your ear to my appeal.
You are faithful, you are just; give answer.
Do not call your servant to judgment
for no one is just in your sight. R.

I remember the days that are past:
I ponder all your works.
I muse on what your hand has wrought
and to you I stretch out my hands. R.

In the morning let me know your love
for I put my trust in you.
Make me know the way I should walk:
to you I lift up my soul. R.

Gospel *Matthew 25:14-23*

Each person here has different personal talents. The gospel story is about using those talents in the service of God.

A reading from the holy Gospel according to Matthew.

The kingdom of heaven is like a man on his way abroad who summoned his servants and entrusted his property to them. To one he gave five talents, to another two, each in proportion to his ability. Then he set out. The man who had received the five talents promptly went and traded with them and made five more. The man who had received two made two more in the same way. The man who had received the five talents came forward bringing five more. 'Sir,' he said 'you entrusted me with five talents; here are five more that I have made.' His master said to him, 'Well done, good and faithful servant; you have shown you can be faithful in small things, I will trust you with greater; come and join in your master's happiness.' Next the man with the two talents came forward. 'Sir,' he said 'you entrusted me with two talents; here are two more that I have made.' His master said to him, 'Well done, good and faithful servant; you have shown you can be faithful in small things, I will trust you with greater; come and join in your master's happiness.'

Prayer of the Faithful

We make our prayer of the faithful; we pray for this group here, and for others who are in our minds:

For ourselves, that we get through these days without undue anxiety, that the support of family and friends will help us in time of stress: Lord hear us.

R. *Lord in your mercy, hear our prayer.*

We pray for our teachers, and for others who help us in school work. Help them in whatever way they need at present: Lord hear us. R.

For anyone who has experienced failure in exams, give them, we pray, confidence in their talents: Lord hear us. R.

For an equality of educational opportunity for every child in our country and in the world. Lord hear us. R.

Let us pray:

We come to you, loving God, in confident prayer.

We know that you accept with joy the service of our talents.

We pray that we may use all our personality in your service.

We ask this through Christ our Lord. Amen.

Prayer over the Gifts
We offer to you God, creator and friend,
all the good desires of our lives.
We want to be people who can love as you love,
who can see in each of us here
a reflection of yourself and your love.
We make this prayer in the name of Jesus the Lord. Amen.

Invitation to Communion
We have not seen Jesus the Christ; yet in faith we believe in him and
we are happy to be called to this Eucharist.
Lord I am not worthy to receive you,
but only say the word and I shall be healed.

Communion Reflection
Each person here is made in the likeness of God.
Each person has special gifts and talents.
As we prepare for our exams,
may we learn to love and accept one another
as we are, and to value the unique abilities each has.
May God be with us, enlighten us and strengthen us,
and relieve our anxieties.

Concluding Prayer
Gracious God, in the celebration of this Eucharist,
you strengthen our faith, enliven our hope, and make our love more
wholehearted. We thank you for this time with you in faith, and we
thank you in the name of Jesus the Lord. Amen.

12. Choosing a Career

Introduction

We've all changed our minds a lot since childhood about what we'd like to do with our lives, what sort of career we'll select. We go through changes of mind, and sometimes we have to accept the limitations of our personalities and talents in thinking of a career. It's an experience we all go through, and it can be very worrying. We want to choose a career and then there are aspects of it we don't like. We wonder should money or people be more important in our choices, and we worry about failure. We know many people who have changed their career, sometimes with a new zest for life and success, other times with regrets for the rest of their lives.

We wonder where God should be in our choices and question whether God has a plan for us. At times we feel very idealistic and want to dedicate our lives to improving the world. We can feel a lot of joy and happiness in being able to choose what we want. For some of us, there is the prospect of unemployment, or the pressure to take whatever we get. And somewhere in it all, our faith calls us to include others and their needs in how we might spend our lives. That's what we'll think about and pray over during Mass, praying for light to know what to do and courage to do it. We'll also pray for each other.

Penitential Rite

As we begin our Mass, we call to mind that we need God's help in our lives and forgiveness of our sins and selfishness.

Lord, you chose to follow the will of your Father:
Lord have mercy.
Lord, you are the Way, the Truth, and the Life:
Christ have mercy.
Lord, you are our God, one with the Father and the Spirit:
Lord have mercy.

Opening Prayer

Loving God, be with us in all we do and say,
think, feel, desire and decide in our lives.
Give each of us light to know our talents
and courage to use them in your service.
Help us find careers suitable to us

where our talents and personalities may develop
and we make this prayer through Christ our Lord. Amen.

First Reading *1 John 2:7-11*
In making life-decisions, God asks us to put love first in our concerns.

A reading from the first letter of John.

Beloved, I am writing you no new commandment, but an old commandment that you have had since the beginning; the old commandment is the word that you have heard. Yet I am writing you a new commandment that is true in him and in you, because the darkness is passing away and the true light is already shining. Whoever says 'I am in the light,' while hating a brother or sister, is still in the darkness. Whoever loves a brother or sister lives in the light, and in such a person there is no cause for stumbling. But whoever hates another believer is in the darkness, walks in the darkness, and does not know the way to go, because the darkness has brought on blindness.

Responsorial Psalm
Psalm 25 A poem to trust in God's nearness when we make choices in life.
RESPONSE: Lord, you are the light of the world.

Lord make me know your ways,
Lord teach me your paths.
Make me walk in your truth and teach me,
for you are God, my Saviour. R

In you I hope all the day long,
because of your goodness, O Lord.
Remember your mercy, O Lord,
and the love you have shown from of old. R.

Gospel *Matthew 16:21-23*
Jesus chose to follow in his life what his Father wanted, even when that meant some opposition from Peter, his own disciple.

A reading from the holy Gospel according to Matthew.

From that time Jesus began to make it clear to his disciples that he was destined to go to Jerusalem and suffer grievously at the hands of the elders and chief priests and scribes, to be put to death and to be raised up on the third day. Then taking him aside, Peter began to remonstrate with him. 'Heaven preserve you, Lord,' he said, 'this must not happen to you.' But he turned and said to Peter, 'Get behind me Satan. You are an obstacle in my path because the way you think is not God's way, but man's.'

Prayer of the Faithful

Let's pray for clarity in knowing and deciding what to do in our lives, for help in a choice of career when we need it, and for everyone here.

For ourselves, Lord, that we may know what career to choose, make good decisions, and help others in what we decide to do in life: Lord hear us.
R Lord, in your faithfulness, hear our prayer.
We ask you that we can grow in love of you, Lord, and of your people, so that our career decisions will always include some care for those less fortunate than ourselves: Lord hear us. R.
We pray for those out of work, especially young people, that their lack of employment won't lead to too much discouragement, and that all our people, especially our churches, may respond to the need for full employment: Lord hear us. R.
We pray, too, that the improvement in technology and machinery won't lead to a devaluing of the dignity of the human person: Lord hear us. R.

Almighty God, we make our prayers to you in faith and hope and love. We make them through Jesus who toiled and worked like everyone else and whose decisions were always made in your light.
We pray in the name of Jesus the Lord. Amen.

Prayer over the Gifts

We pray, God our Father, that our offering in this Mass
may help us know Jesus your Son
who is a friend to us in our lives.
In all our questions and decisions
may we find him trustworthy and caring for us,
for he is the certainty of your love,
now and forever.

Communion Reflection

Making a decision can be a lonely time;
I can take advice and talk with friends;
I can ask someone who has travelled that path before;
I can pray and think and wonder what is the right choice.
But there seem to be times when I cannot say to anyone else

what's really in my mind and heart.
It's like trying to go both directions at a crossroads
or it's like being in the dark with only the glimmer of a candle,
or like a day when the clouds blot out the sun.
I question, wonder, hope, feel strongly, doubt,
all the bits and pieces of a decision.
I am alone, but not fully alone,
for God is always with me,
the listener, the one who calms all anxiety.
God travels with us
a light in the dark night,
in the cloud by day.
Let's pray for belief in God's presence,
and not be afraid of the dark or the cloud;
and let God be the way to guide us
at whatever crossroads we find
when we are making the important decisions of our lives.

Concluding Prayer
Loving God, be with us, we ask you, all the days of our future.
May we help each other with sincerity and truthfulness
as we make decisions that effect our lives.
And may we offer our talents and gifts
in the service of your people,
through Jesus Christ our Lord. Amen.

13. Death of a Young Person

Introduction

Death is always a shock; even more so when it's the death of a young person, known to us for either a short or long time. We have many words and few words: many words to say what's unimportant and few words to say the real, caring things we'd like to say to each other. We come here to remember a young person, to give thanks, even in our grief, for his/her life, to offer each other, and especially those who will most miss him/her, the consolation of our love and presence; and to offer also the promise of eternal life. Our consolations will be the joyful memories we have; our sadness is that a young person has gone from us at an age we did not expect. Our sure hope is that the Lord our God will welcome him/her home, and that one day we will be united together in heaven. In the depth of our loss and hope we now pray and offer the sacrifice and thanksgiving of Jesus to his Father.

Penitential Rite

We come to God, knowing we need mercy and forgiveness, and so in preparing to celebrate the Mass we call to mind our sins:
I confess ...

Opening Prayer

Loving God, source of all life, in this world and the next,
we pray to you for our dear brother/sister ...
Welcome him/her to the eternal joy of your kingdom
and give us all new hope in our sorrow
that one day we shall all be with you and with each other
in your home where every tear will be wiped away.
Grant this, we ask you, through Jesus Christ our Lord.

First Reading *Isaiah 55:6-11*

This passage from Isaiah is a confident statement of belief that nothing of what God makes or does is wasted, but is part of a loving plan.

A reading from the prophet Isaiah.

Seek the Lord while he is still to be found,
call to him while he is still near.
Let the wicked man abandon his ways,
the evil man his thoughts.

Let him turn back to the Lord who will take pity on him,
for my thoughts are not your thoughts,
my ways not your ways – it is the Lord who speaks.
Yes, the heavens are high above the earth
as my ways are above your ways,
my thoughts are above your thoughts.

Yes, as the rain and the snow come down from the heavens and do not return without watering the earth, making it yield and giving growth to provide seed for the sower and bread for the eating, so the word that goes from my mouth does not return to me empty, without carrying out my will and succeeding in what it was sent to do.

Responsorial Psalm
Psalm 24 This is a poem of trust in God's ultimate call.
RESPONSE: This day you will be with me in paradise.
Lord, make your ways known to me,
teach me your paths.
Set me in the way of your truth, and teach me,
for you are the God who saves me. R.

All day long I hope in you
because of your goodness, O Lord.
Remember your kindness, Lord,
your love, which you showed long ago.
Do not remember the sins of my youth,
but rather, with your love remember me. R.

Relieve the distress of my heart,
free me from my sufferings,
forgive all my sins. R.

Gospel *Luke 24:1-8*
> *We listen to the story of the resurrection of Jesus: this is the story which will give hope and consolation to us at the time of death. It is the reminder that everyone's life is for this world and the next. Our sure hope is that he/she who has died will share in this risen life of Jesus Christ.*

A reading from the holy Gospel according to Luke.

On the first day of the week, at the first sign of dawn, they went to the tomb with the spices they had prepared. They found that the stone had been rolled away from the tomb, but on entering discovered that the body of the Lord Jesus was not there. As they stood there not knowing what to think, two men in brilliant clothes suddenly appeared at their side. Terrified, the women lowered their eyes. But the two men said to them, 'Why look among the dead for someone who is alive? He is not here; he has risen. Remember what he told you when he was still in Galilee: that the Son of Man had to be handed over into the power of sinful men and be crucified, and rise again on the third day.' And they remembered his words.

Prayer of the Faithful

Let us pray now to God, the source of life; we pray for our friend who has died and also for those who mourn him/her; for ourselves and for all God's people.

Give eternal rest to _____, and may the light of Jesus Christ shine upon him/her. Lord, hear us.
Response: Lord, graciously hear us.

Give to those who mourn him/her and will miss him/her the hope that he/she is with God, and let them always be thankful for the good of his/her life. Lord hear us. R.

We pray for all we know who have died, for family and friends; we pray especially for those who have died unmourned and unloved, Lord hear us. R.

We remember those who are widowed and all families who have lost a parent; may God console them with love, Lord hear us. R.

For those who have died in the cause of justice and of faith, we pray to the Lord. Lord hear us. R.

Grant to us, gracious God, a strong confidence
that you are God of the living,
and that nothing you have made is forgotten
in your sight and in your love.
We ask this through Christ our Lord. Amen.

Prayer over the Gifts

Gracious God, Father of our Lord and Brother, Jesus Christ,
we give to you in bread and wine
the sadness at our loss and our thanks for _____.
May we all grow in hope this day
as we pray with him/her and all who have gone before us,
who have shared in the Bread of Life at your table.
We ask this in the name of Jesus the Lord. Amen.

Invitation to Communion
This is the body of the risen Lord, which we gratefully receive in memory of _____, and in our hope of eternal life. We are happy to be called to this Eucharist.

Communion Reflection
We can look on death in many ways:
a cloud that is dark,
a moment of intense aloneness,
a stinging fear,
an experience we resist and
don't want to talk about.
We cannot avoid it nor escape it;
our experience this day
reminds us that death is a moment we all will face.
Can we see in it the outstretched hand of God,
the light beyond the cloud that is dark;
or the companionship of Christ Jesus in this
fearful moment of aloneness?
As loved ones who have died in the peace of Christ
beckoned us into life,
they beckon us, too, from beyond this earthly life,
to share in the light and love of Jesus,
whose death was the beginning
of the risen life on Easter morning.

Concluding Prayer
Almighty God, your gift of the Body and Blood of Christ
is a sign of your unending love for your people.
May we be strengthened in our loss,
may we be encouraged in the darkness of death
and live our lives in service of you
as we hope to share in the risen life of Christ.
We make our prayer through Christ our Lord. Amen.

14. Mass for the End of School

Introduction

We're here today to remember, to pray and to think in hope about the future. We're at Mass to thank God for our times together, for the friends we have made, for all we've learned about life from teachers and from each other. We're here, too, so that we can pray for each other, each one's happiness in the future. This is a time of some sadness and some joy—sad to leave a lot behind, but joy in moving on. We pray also for ourselves in the coming exams, for peace of mind and for success in them. We look ahead in hope and know that God will be with us in the future as God has companioned us up to now. With a sense of joy and of thanks, we now begin our Mass.

Penitential Rite

We ask God's forgiveness for sin, especially for the ways we have been unkind to others and neglectful of God and ungrateful.

Lord, you have come to call sinners to yourself:
Lord have mercy. R.
Lord, you forgave all who hurt you:
Christ have mercy. R.
You plead for us at the right hand of the Father:
Lord have mercy. R.

Opening Prayer

We thank you, gracious God, for the gifts of life and of love;
we thank you for the gifts of learning and of intelligence.
We ask you that you will always help us
to use these gifts in your service.
Give us a lively faith in you
that will be stronger than any doubts we have,
a hope that will take us through any hard times of life,
and a love that is sincere as we give ourselves in your service.
We ask this through Christ our Lord. Amen.

First Reading *2 Thessalonians 2:13-3:16*

This reading is an encouragement from Paul to his people to be faithful to all they had learned from him, and to their faith. It is a prayer we might make for each other as we celebrate the end of our time together.

A reading from Paul to the Thessalonians.

But we feel we must be continually thanking God for you, whom the Lord loves, because God chose you from the beginning to be saved by the sanctifying Spirit and by faith in the truth. Through the Good News that he brought he called you to this so that you should share the glory of our Lord Jesus Christ. Stand firm, then, and keep the traditions that we taught you.

May our Lord Jesus Christ himself, and God our Father who has given us his love and such sure hope, comfort you and strengthen you in everything good that you do or say. Finally pray that the Lord's message may spread quickly and be received with honor as it was among you ... But the Lord is faithful and he will give you strength and guard you from the evil one, and we have every confidence that you are doing and will go on doing all that we tell you. May the Lord turn your hearts towards the love of God and the fortitude of Christ. May the Lord of peace himself give you peace all the time and in every way. The Lord be with you all.

Responsorial Psalm
Psalm 27 This is a song of hope that God will always be with us.
RESPONSE: The Lord is with us all the days of our life.

The Lord is my light and my shield,
whom shall I fear?
The Lord is the stronghold of my life,
against whom shall I be afraid? R.

I believe I shall see the Lord's goodness
in the land of the living.
Hope in God, hold firm and take heart,
Hope in the Lord. R.

Gospel *Luke 24:28-31*
After a journey with his disciples Jesus breaks the bread with them. This action of Christ, repeated in every Mass, is his promise and our certainty that he is with us always. We hear that promise today as we leave school.

A reading from the holy Gospel according to Luke.

When they drew near to the village to which they were going, he made as if to go on: but they pressed him to stay with them. 'It is nearly evening' they said 'and the day is almost over.' So he went in to stay with them. Now while he was with them at table, he took the bread and said the blessing; then broke it and handed it to them. And their eyes were opened and they recognized him.

Prayer of the Faithful
We look now to the future and pray for everyone here, and for other intentions we remember.

Give good health, happiness and love to everyone here. Lord hear our prayer.
Response: Lord in your faithfulness, hear our prayer.
May everyone here find a job that gives satisfaction in their lives, may they find friendship and joy, and courage in times that are difficult. Lord hear our prayer. R.
Give us Lord, a sense of commitment in life; may we find our way of serving you in life, and use our talents for the good of others. Lord hear our prayer. R.
For anyone in our class who is sick, for those who are over-anxious about exams, for those who have died. We remember them and others who come to mind now. Lord hear our prayer. R.

Prayer over the Gifts
Gracious God, may our prayer together
increase our faith in your companionship,
our hope in your love,
our love for your people.
As we offer this bread and wine,
may we be strengthened in our friendship with you,
now and forever.
We ask this through Jesus the Lord. Amen.

Communion Reflection
Our lives are marked forever
by those we meet;
the friendships we make and the love we experience,
the reconciliations and the quarrels,
the works we have tried to do together,
for each other and for those less fortunate.
All this has given us something that will last.

Long after we've forgotten the marks of our exams,
we'll remember the friendships, the times of growth,

the fun, the laughter, the jokes.
We'll remember how we helped each other to grow as people,
in faith, in hope and in love.
May what we have done in this place
be given to many others in our lives.

Concluding Prayer
God our Father, bless us as we go from this table of your love,
and from this place where you have been present among us.
Bless all those who have given their time to us;
bless all those who work here, teachers and staff.
May we go forth from here, confident in ourselves,
and willing to serve others.
We make this prayer through Christ our Lord. Amen.

15. Growth of Faith

Introduction

A writer states: 'Faith is a gift from God, as fragile as a flower in the desert that needs to be watered and cultivated. This cultivation is even more important in a society and culture that tend to speak less and less about faith.'

The way we think about God and our prayer changes as we get older. We get new questions, and experiences in life make us ask different things of God. Sometimes people panic that they are losing their faith when in fact their faith is growing. It's something like friendship or any relationship: what we were happy about as children doesn't satisfy us in the teens, and what is a good friendship in the teens won't satisfy us in adult life.

We can sometimes get very negative about faith. Different people can give a bad impression of Christianity. But that shouldn't keep anyone from growing towards God themselves. Our faith is affected by the faith and lives of others, but it is an intensely personal experience. Jesus himself got to know God gradually in his life: through the Jewish religion, through his mother and Joseph. He got to know the God inside himself.

We pray at this Mass that our faith may be honest, sincere and open to growth. And we pray for the faith of each person here, that it can be a life-giving relationship in their lives.

Penitential Rite

As we prepare to celebrate the mystery of God's love, we ask for the gifts of forgiveness and love in our lives.

You are the Way to true life and to God in heaven:
Lord have mercy.
You are the Truth of our questions and the love of God:
Christ have mercy.
You are the Life of God and the meaning of human life:
Lord have mercy.

Opening Prayer

Help our faith to grow, gracious God.
We ask that we may know you
as the Way, the Truth and the Life.

Grant this through Christ our Lord. Amen.

First Reading *Colossians 3:1-4*

The life of faith is a life focused on God and looking at the world the way God sees the world. It is mysterious; we will only fully know God in the life that is to come.

A reading from the letter of Paul to the Colossians.

Since you have been brought back to true life with Christ, you must look for the things that are in heaven, where Christ is, sitting at God's right hand. Let your thoughts be on heavenly things, not on things that are on the earth, because you have died, and now the life you have is hidden with Christ in God. But when Christ is revealed, he is your life and you, too, will be revealed in all your glory with him.

Responsorial Psalm

Psalm 86 A prayer for the care of God.
RESPONSE: Lord I believe, help my unbelief.

Listen to me, Lord my God, and answer me,
poor and needy as I am; keep me safe,
I am your devoted one,
save your servant who relies on you. R.

You are my God, take pity on me,
Lord, I pray to you all day long;
give me reason to rejoice,
for to you, Lord, I lift up my soul. R.

Gospel *Luke 2:41-52*

In this story Jesus loses his father and mother and finds God; but he also returns with his parents to their home and finds God there also. Faith is a personal search for God and God's truth and love within a community of believers.

A reading from the holy Gospel according to Luke.

Every year his parents used to go to Jerusalem for the feast of the Passover. When he was twelve years old, they went up for the feast as usual. When they were on their way home after the feast, the boy Jesus stayed behind in Jerusalem without his parents knowing it. They assumed he was with the caravan, and it was only after a day's journey that they went to look for him among their relations and acquaintances. When they failed to find him there they went back to

Jerusalem looking for him everywhere.

Three days later, they found him in the Temple, sitting among the doctors, listening to them and asking them questions; and all those who heard him were astounded at his intelligence and his replies. They were overcome when they saw him and his mother said to him, 'My child, why have you done this to us? See how worried your father and I have been, looking for you.' 'Why were you looking for me?' he replied, 'Did you not know that I must be busy with my father's affairs?' But they did not understand what he meant.

He then went down with them and came to Nazareth, and lived under their authority. His mother stored up all these things in her heart. And Jesus increased in wisdom, stature, and in favour with God and people.

Prayer of the Faithful
We bring our prayers to God in faith and in trust that God hears what we ask:
> Deepen our faith; help us to be honest in our questions and humbly to accept that we don't have all the answers; Lord, hear us.
> Give faith and hope to young people who are confused; we pray that we can help our friends in times when they feel lost and abandoned; Lord, hear us.
> Give courage and strength to people who are imprisoned or oppressed in any way because of their faith in you; Lord, hear us.
> For people who are trying to help others in their life of faith, particularly parents and teachers; Lord, hear us.

Let us pray:
Gracious God, we pray these intentions of our hearts.
We believe in your care for us.
Help us remember this all the days of our life.
We ask this through Christ our Lord. Amen.

Prayer over the Gifts
We bring these gifts of bread and wine in faith to you;
we know that they come from you, source of all life.
May they bring us to a loving faith in your care for us.
We ask this through Christ our Lord. Amen.

Communion Reflection
If Jesus said, 'Blessed are the poor in spirit',
it was because of his conviction,

born out of his own life
and learned through the experience of men and women he met,
that the poor in spirit are blessed, content, and happy.
Maybe he listened for hours to a woman
who was really humble and open about her lack of success and pres-
tige, but found her happier than many a society lady of leisure,
because she had found the meaning of her life in God and in love;
or maybe he spent time with a man who grappled with frailty
or struggled with a weakness like alcoholism,
and realized that deep down this man had a contentment
in a humble approach to his own weakness,
and he knew that his own fulfilment and contentment
was in being totally dependent on God
for life, love, happiness, perseverance,and a sense of purpose ...
then he could say, 'I live, as I was born, poor in spirit, and I am
blessed.'

Concluding Prayer
God our Creator and Father,
may our minds be open to the Truth we hear in Jesus,
may our hearts be open to his Life,
and may our feet be guided always on his Way,
the path of faith on our journey of life.
We ask this through Christ our Lord. Amen.

16. Being a Christian

Introduction

Our Mass today is on the theme of being a Christian. We want to pray and think over the essentials of following Christ.

One main aspect of our Christianity is that we try to look at the world as Jesus did. A word that sums up Christianity is love. This is how Jesus would distinguish his disciples. Many people look at Christianity in different ways: stressing prayer, social action, sacraments, devotions, and morality. All are important, but none more important than love. Jesus showed this in his life.

Michel Quoist, a French writer, puts it well: 'What distinguishes the Christian from the non-Christian? Nothing. The Christian is no better or no worse; he [sic] is no more virtuous than the others; in fact he might even be less so. No more loving or giving than anyone else; there are people who love more. There's only one difference: as a Christian you believe that God loves you and that if you welcome this love, it will be transmitted to the world through you, and on this love the world will be built.'

Penitential Rite

Jesus asks us to confess that we are people who fail to love, and asks us to allow God's forgiveness into our lives.

Lord Jesus, you are the Truth of God our Father:
Lord have mercy.
Lord Jesus, you are the Life of forgiveness and reconciliation:
Christ have mercy.
Lord Jesus, you are the Way to love and joy:
Lord have mercy.
May almighty God have mercy on us, forgive us our sins, and bring us to life everlasting. Amen.

Opening Prayer

God our Father,
make us truly grateful for the gift of our faith.
It gives hope and meaning to our lives.
Deepen our Christianity, and help us to share it.
We ask this through Christ Our Lord. Amen.

First Reading *Hebrews 10:19-25*
   This reading stresses different aspects of being a Christian.

A reading from the letter of Paul to the Hebrews.

Through the blood of Jesus we have a right to enter the sanctuary, by a new way which he has opened for us. And we have the supreme high priest over all the house of God. So as we go in, let us be sincere in heart and filled with faith, our minds free from any trace of bad conscience and our bodies washed with pure water. Let us keep firm in the hope we profess, because the one who made the promise is faithful. Let us be concerned for each other, to stir a response in love and good works. Do not stay away from the meetings of the community, as some do, but encourage each other to go.

Responsorial Psalm
Psalm 111 A poem about trusting in God and giving to the poor.
RESPONSE: We thank you God for the gift of our faith.

Happy those who fear the Lord,
who take delight in his commands;
their children will be blessed on earth;
the children of the upright will be blessed. R.

Open handed they give to the poor;
their justice stands firm for ever.
They will be raised in glory. R.

Gospel *Luke 10:25-28*
   In this gospel Jesus sums up the Christian message in three aspects: love of each other, of self and of God.

A reading from the holy Gospel according to Luke.

A lawyer stood up to test Jesus. 'Teacher', he said, 'what must I do to inherit eternal life?' He said to him, 'What is written in the law? What do you read there? He answered, 'You shall love your God with all your heart, and with all your soul, and with all your strength, and with all your mind; and your neighbor as yourself.' And he said to him, 'You have given the right answer; do this and you will live.'

Prayer of the Faithful
With thanks to God, let us pray and make our intentions:
   As we thank God for the gift of faith, we pray for an increase of faith and love in our own lives; Lord, hear us.

We ask God's help and care for people, especially young people,
who find it difficult to believe. Help them in their doubts; Lord,
hear us.

We pray for people who are in prison or suffering any oppression
because of their efforts to spread the gospel of Jesus; Lord, hear us.

We pray for anyone who has helped in giving us the gift of faith
and of Christianity: our parents, teachers, friends; Lord, hear us,

We pray for priests, sisters, brothers, and all who are ministers of religion. May God bless them in their work; Lord, hear us.

Let us pray:

Gracious God, deepen within us our faith in you.

Give us joy in the efforts of Christians,

all over the world, to spread your gospel.

We ask this through Christ our Lord. Amen.

Prayer over the Gifts

May our small gifts of bread and wine, loving God,

be the gifts of our hearts.

Make us joyful in your love of us,

and intent on giving the world your gospel of love

and of reconciliation.

We ask this in the name of Christ the Lord. Amen.

Communion Reflection

I welcome you, Lord, into my life;

and work of my life,

into my hopes and fears.

I welcome you thankfully

because you are a friend,

because you accept me, as you accept us all,

because you are forgiving.

Lord, help me to learn from you,

to learn that God is friend and father,

to learn that I am worth God's love and worth your death;

help me to learn from you how to love,

how to live in your love,

acting and forgiving others in turn.

This, Lord, is my prayer,

to be like you and not lose myself in the process:

to be the person you have made

and grow into to the man or woman you are shaping;
help me to live for you, to work with you,
to share your gospel of peace and love
with my own unique personality,
unlike anyone else's.

Thank you, Lord, for your friendship,
thank you for what I learn from you,
thank you that at this moment I can call you
Friend, Teacher, Lord and God.

Concluding Prayer
We go from this place, God our Father,
strengthened by the body and blood of Jesus.
In the Eucharist, may we always know your love
and your call in our lives.
Thank you for being so close to us.
We make this prayer through Christ our Lord. Amen.

17. Living in Hope

Introduction
We live in a world and among people who seem to lose hope. Yet the Gospel of Jesus promises hope and joy, both in this world and the next. Many of the problems of both young and old people today spring from a lack of hope. People on drugs or in depression, who sometimes feel like suicide, or who sometimes just feel down, may be lacking in hope. We look at the whole world we're in and we see unemployment, nuclear threats, breakdown of marriage and other relationships, and we wonder how we can hope.

The hope that Jesus offers spreads from him through others; we can be signs of hope to each other. Hope in our courage and in our optimism. Hope springing from the love of God which is always a reality, no matter how much it might seem otherwise. Where injustices are challenged, where love wins out, where courage is a motivating force, then the hope of the Gospel, seen in the promises and life of Jesus, becomes a reality.

We'll think and pray over this in our Mass today.

Penitential Rite
We ask God's forgiveness for our sins against hope, particularly for ways in which we have been discouraging to others when they were trying to be enthusiastic and optimistic in face of difficulties.

Lord Jesus, you send us the Spirit of hope:
Lord have mercy.
Lord Jesus, you are the sign of the Father's eternal love:
Christ have mercy.
Lord Jesus, you are our hope in the presence of God:
Lord have mercy.

Opening Prayer
Almighty God, hope of all your people,
we open our hearts now to your love and to your hopes for us.
You have hopes for your people:
that we can create in your world a place of justice
and in your people a heart of compassion and love.
We ask you now that your love will be the source of our hope.
We ask this through Christ the Lord. Amen.

First Reading *Isaiah 35:1-7, 10*

A picture of hope in the Bible is water flowing and flowers growing in a desert. Maybe we can stretch that imagery to a desert where food will grow once again, and to hearts where hope will drive us to love and help others.

A reading from the prophet Isaiah.

Let the wilderness and dry lands exult,
let the wasteland rejoice and bloom,
let it bring forth flowers and sing for joy.

Strengthen all weary hands,
steady all trembling knees
and say to all faint hearts,
'Courage, do not be afraid.
Look, your God is coming,
coming to save you.'

Then the eyes of the blind shall be opened,
the ears of the deaf unsealed,
then shall the lame leap like deer,
and the tongues of the dumb sing for joy;

for water gushes in the desert,
streams in the wasteland,
the scorched earth becomes a lake,
the parched lands become springs of water.

Responsorial Psalm
*Psalm 27 In this psalm the poet gets hope and courage
from the trustworthiness of God.*
RESPONSE: Lord we hope because of your promise of friendship.

The Lord is my light and my help, whom shall I fear?
The Lord is the stronghold of my life;
before whom shall I shrink? R

There is one thing I ask of the Lord, for this I long,
to live in the house of the Lord,
all the days of my life,
to enjoy the friendship of the Lord,
to live in his presence. R

Gospel *Mark 16:9-20*

The hope of a Christian is based on the goodness of God, the love possible between human beings, and the resurrection of Jesus. This account of the resurrection grounds our faith in Jesus and also indicates that through his apostles and followers he offers hope to the world.

A reading from the holy Gospel according to Mark.

Having risen in the morning on the first day of the week, he appeared first to Mary of Magdala from whom he had cast out seven devils. She then went to those who had been his companions, and who were mourning and in tears, and told them. But they did not believe her when they heard her say that he was alive and that she had seen him.

After this, he showed himself under another form to two of them as they were on their way into the country. These went back and told the others, who did not believe them either.

Lastly, he showed himself to the Eleven themselves while they were at the table. He reproached them for their incredulity and obstinacy, because they had refused to believe those who had seen him after he had risen. And he said to them, 'Go out to the whole world; proclaim the Good News to all creation.'

And so the Lord Jesus, after had spoken to them, was taken up into heaven; there at the right hand of God he took his place, while they, going out, preached everywhere, the Lord working with them and confirming the word by signs that accompanied it.

Prayer of the Faithful

We'll pray now to God, especially for people who seem to lack hope in their lives, and for our world which also seems to lack hope, asking God that the hope of the Gospel will be more evident among people.

Give us your gift of hope, Lord, hope in the goodness of your people, through all the troubles and frustrations of life, because you are stronger than any evil in the world: Lord hear us.

For young people who seem to be despairing, who turn to shallow relationships, or to success for their meaning in life, and for those whose lives are painfully affected by any form of drug addiction: Lord hear us.

We remember many things that frighten people today: violence, nuclear build-up, family problems, and we ask you to create places of hope among people: Lord hear us.

May your church be a sign of hope. Don't let your people lose hope and enthusiasm, and help the leaders of all churches to be witnesses of hope and optimism: Lord hear us.

Loving God, we thank you for the gift of hope.

Help us to show our thanks by spreading hope in our world, through our Lord, Jesus Christ. Amen.

Offertory

Place some symbols of hope on the altar. The Bible and a candle with it could be central; other signs would be a cassette tape of hope-filled music, a ring, a flower; a picture of someone who embodies hope, a grain of wheat, a sign of food for the hungry.

Prayer over the Gifts

Gracious God, we have gathered around
this table of your friendship.
In thanks and in hope we pray to you
that our sharing in this Mass
may make us better friends to each other
and to those we will meet in the years ahead.
May we be men and women who will spread in our world
friendship based on the friendship of Christ,
who is Lord forever and ever. Amen.

Invitation to Communion

This is the bread of hope. When we welcome it into our lives, we welcome the gift of hope and the challenge to be followers of Jesus. We are happy to be called to this Eucharist.

Lord I am not worthy to receive you,
but only say the word and I shall be healed.

Communion Reflection

Hope is like a flower or a river;
color rooted in God's creation;
movement and flow from the source that is God.
It's also like a bridge,
linking our fears and God's faithfulness,
and the foundation is the promise of God.
And it's more:
it's the smile in the midst of a crowd,
the touch of sympathy and understanding,
a joke or story that's shared,

a prayer that shifts the winds of worry and desire;
all in all, it's sharing in the love of God,
color, water, pathway in the desert
or the wasteland.
And it's thanks from the heart.

Concluding Prayer

God our Father, you call us to this table of thanksgiving;
you invite us to share in your call to justice and hope,
for these are the signs of your kingdom
and the work of your Spirit present among us.
We ask you that we can go from this place
and find you in all the circumstances of our lives,
so that we are a people of thanksgiving and hope.
This we ask in the name of Christ the Lord. Amen.

18. Self-Image

Introduction

We all go through times of feeling good and bad about ourselves. You can sometimes feel like you're in a 'hall of mirrors' – look one way and you're fat, another and you're thin, another and you're tall. Everywhere you look, you look different. Most of us feel different with different people, maybe shy with adults and confident with peers. We have a sense of our value and lovableness when we're with a friend, and with someone else we can feel very inferior. We wonder which is the 'real me', and it's important that we find out.

The main word for our relationship with Jesus is friendship and friendship gives us a good sense of ourselves. That's now what we'll pray about during this Mass together. And we'll pray that we can see ourselves as God sees us, and treat each other like that.

Penitential Rite

We often need the friendship of Christ to let us know that we are lovable. We pray now, not just for forgiveness but for healing. We pray that Christ may let us know that he does love us, and that he can heal the memory of times in the past when our good sense of ourselves was injured.

Lord Jesus, you have called us to be friends:
Lord have mercy.
Christ our Lord, we are created in God's image and likeness:
Christ have mercy.
Lord Jesus, we believe in the goodness of everyone:
Lord have mercy.

Opening Prayer

God our Father, you are the source of all life,
and the source of all love.
You have created and formed each person here
with the loving hand of care and the caring heart of friendship.
We ask you now to strengthen our belief
in the value and worth we each have in your sight.
We ask this through Christ the Lord. Amen.

First Reading *2 Corinthians 12:7-10*

> *Paul writes about sensing two sides of himself: the strong and the weak. Both are part of him like both are part of each of us. He sees his weakness and strength as important in his friendship with Christ. He looks at himself and sees Christ accepting him fully.*

A reading from the second letter to the Corinthians.

In view of the extraordinary nature of these revelations, to stop me from getting too proud I was given a thorn in the flesh, an angel of Satan to beat me and stop me from getting too proud! About this thing, I have pleaded with the Lord three times for it to leave me, but he has said, 'My grace is enough for you: my power is at its best in weakness.' So I shall be very happy to make my weaknesses my special boast so that the power of Christ may stay over me, and this is why I am quite content with my weaknesses, and with insults, hardships, persecutions, and the agonies I go through for Christ's sake. For it is when I am weak that I am strong.

Responsorial Psalm

Psalm 139 A poem about God's knowing each of us.
RESPONSE: I thank you for the wonder of my being.

It was you who created my being,
knit me together in my mother's womb.
I thank you for the wonder of my being,
for the wonders of all your creation. R.

Already you knew my soul,
my body held no secret from you,
when I was being fashioned in secret
and moulded in the depths of the earth. R.

O search me, God, and know my heart.
O test me and know my thoughts.
See that I follow not the wrong path
and lead me in the path of life eternal. R.

Gospel *Luke 5:1-11*

> *Peter had an experience of different sides of himself when he met Jesus and for a while he thought he was 'all bad'. In that very moment Jesus saw other sides to him, and in both the good and bad sides of him that he saw, he called him as an apostle.*

A reading from the holy Gospel according to Luke.

Jesus was standing one day by the lake of Gennesaret, with the crowd pressing around him listening to the word of God, when he caught sight of two boats close to the bank. The fishermen had gone out of them and were washing their nets. He got into one of the boats—it was Simon's—and asked him to put out a little from the shore. Then he sat down and taught the crowds from the boat.

When he had finished speaking, he said to Simon, 'Put out into deep water and lay out your nets for a catch.' 'Master,' Simon replied 'we worked hard all night long and caught nothing, but if you say so, I will lay out the nets.' And when they had done this they netted such a huge number of fish that their nets began to tear, so they signalled to their companions in the other boats to come and help them; when these came, they filled the two boats to sinking point.

When Simon Peter saw this he fell at the knees of Jesus saying, 'Leave me, Lord; I am a sinful man.' But Jesus said to Simon, 'Do not be afraid; from now on it is people you will catch.' Then, bringing their boats back to land, they left everything and followed him.

Prayer of the Faithful
We pray now for a good sense of ourselves, and especially for people who suffer a lot in life because they see themselves as of little value.

Help each person here, Lord Christ, to see himself/herself reflected in your eyes, as you see us as infinitely lovable in your sight: Lord hear us.

Lord, don't let our guilt and our failures block us from believing in your love and acceptance of ourselves: Lord hear us.

We remember people, especially young people, who turn to drugs, drink, casual relationships to bolster their image of themselves. Lord, may we try in our friendships to give others a good sense of themselves: Lord hear us.

God, Father and friend, we pray that nothing in us will prevent us knowing that you are one who loves. Help us make friendships in which we fully accept each other. Bless all our efforts to build each other up, to speak honestly together, to grow as people created and formed in your love. This we ask through Jesus Christ, our Lord. Amen.

Prayer over the Gifts
We offer to you God, creator and friend,
all the good desires of our lives.
We want to be people who can love as you love,

who can see in each of us here
a reflection of yourself and your love.
We make our prayer through Christ our Lord. Amen.

Communion Reflection

I often wonder which is the real me?
The super confident talker with some people,
the shy, inferior self I find with others,
the carefree, generous self at another time.
Which 'me' do I bring to God?
The confident or the guilty?

My 'self' can be like a sky I wander in,
cloudy one day, bright another.
Which is the real me?
I am a mixture of different moods and thoughts,
changing views of myself and opinions of others.
Lord, help me believe that this is the 'me' that you love,
that you say 'friend' to everything that is me.

Concluding Prayer

Bless us, God our Father, as we leave this gathering.
May we know that you are close to us in love and friendship,
affirming what is good in us and calling us
into a life of friendship and love with you.
May we give to others a true sense of their own value.
We ask this in the name of Christ the Lord. Amen.

19. Self-Acceptance

Introduction

When we look at ourselves and think what sort of people we are, we know we have a good and a bad side. We have qualities we like and qualities we don't like. We have qualities others like and don't like. We can be discouraged at times because we don't like who we are. Or other times we feel very confident, joyful at who we are, especially when someone else accepts us easily.

We are often impatient; we want to be strong overnight, make relationships quickly, achieve easily. But the best things in life grow slowly and with fits and starts. We sometimes learn by mistakes. That's all part of what we'll pray over during the Mass now. By listening to a message of hope and confidence about ourselves, maybe we'll be less hard on ourselves and on others.

Penitential Rite

We're often very impatient with the type of people we are; we want to be different and better. The Gospel of Jesus invites us always to grow and to become stronger in love, but it also invites us to be patient with ourselves and with others. So we pray now, asking God's forgiveness for our selfishness and our impatience with others.

Lord Jesus, you grew in wisdom and in humanity:
Lord have mercy.
Lord Jesus, you were patient with the faults of others:
Christ have mercy.
Lord Jesus, you are our hope and our joy with God our Father:
Lord have mercy.

Opening Prayer

We ask you, loving God,
that the strength of our personalities
be nourished and grow in our relationships with each other,
and that our faults and weaknesses also be used in your service.
You are the one who can bring good out of everything;
help us to be humble and sincere in our attitudes to others,
not intolerant and critical.
This we ask through Christ our Lord. Amen.

First Reading *Isaiah 43:1-7*

In this Scripture God simply tells us that we are precious and loved. Maybe God's love will give us confidence in ourselves. No matter how insecure we may feel, God still loves us.

A reading from the book of Isaiah.

Do not be afraid, for I have redeemed you;
I have called you by your name, you are mine.
Should you pass through the sea, I will be with you;
or through rivers, they will not swallow you up.
Should you walk through fire, you will not be scorched
and the flames will not burn you.
For I am your God,
the Holy One of Israel, your saviour.

You are precious in my eyes,
you are honored and I love you.
Do not be afraid, for I am with you.

Responsorial Psalm
Psalm 139 A poem of joy in accepting oneself.
RESPONSE: I thank you for the wonder of my being.

O Lord, you search me and you know me,
you know my resting and my rising,
you discern my purpose from afar.
You mark when I walk or lie down,
all my ways lie open to you. R.

Before ever a word is on my tongue
you know it, O Lord, through and through.
Too wonderful for me, this knowledge,
too high, beyond my reach. R.

For it was you who created my being,
knit me together in my mother's womb.
I thank you for the wonder of my being,
for the wonders of all your creation. R.

Gospel *Matthew 13:24-30*

This is the story of a field of flowers and weeds; it's a story where Jesus tells us to be patient with growth and development, that it doesn't always happen the way it's planned. We learn from mistakes and through hurt.

A reading from the holy Gospel according to Matthew.

Jesus put another parable before them, 'The kingdom of heaven may be compared to a farmer who sowed good seed in a field. While everybody was asleep an enemy came, sowed weeds all among the wheat, and made off. When the new wheat sprouted and ripened, the weeds appeared as well. The farmer's servants asked, 'Was it not good seed that you sowed in your field? If so, where do the weeds come from?' 'Some enemy has done this,' the farmer answered. And the servants said, 'Do you want us to go and weed it out?' 'No,' the farmer answered, 'because when you weed out the weeds you might pull up the wheat with it. Let them both grow till the harvest; and at harvest time I shall say to the reapers: First collect the weeds and tie them in bundles to be burned, then gather the wheat into my barn.'

Prayer of the Faithful
Let's pray to God for our intentions and for the needs of the world as we see them.

Give us patience, God our Father, with how others grow and develop; help us not to be over-critical of their weaknesses: Lord hear us.
Response: Lord, in your goodness, hear our prayer.
We pray for our parents and families. We know them well and experience so easily their good points and bad points. Help us to be understanding and kind: Lord hear us. R.
For all those in our Church and in our world who are trying to ease famine, homelessness, unemployment in our times. May they not be discouraged by failure but encouraged by the good they do: Lord hear us. R.

Gracious God, we thank you because you care for us, and love each of us in a special, unique relationship. Help us to mirror your love for us in our acceptance of each other, and in our willingness to forgive. We ask this through Christ our Lord. Amen.

Prayer over Gifts
Accept our gift, loving God, we pray,
and give to us the friendship of Jesus, who has come among us
to offer love to the poor and the deprived in our world.
May our hearts be open in trust and in compassion
to spread your justice and love in our world.
We ask this in the name of Christ the Lord. Amen.

Communion Reflection

In each man and woman, of every age, of every race,
God has planted desires for reaching outside ourselves in love.
We want love and truth,
we want to live with courage.
We want to be able to love like a child,
be sympathetic to those in trouble,
and care for the old.
Often through fear,
our self-centered, sometimes violent side
expresses itself in carelessness about others.
We need friends and we need love
to grow into what God wants us to be.
God looks at us and sees the total self,
and sees the possibility there
of creating something beautiful in each of us.

Concluding Prayer

We thank you, gracious God, for the gift of Jesus
who gives meaning to our lives.
May our prayer together at this table give us a sense of our own
goodness and confidence to believe in all this and share it with others.
We ask this through Jesus who is Lord. Amen.

20. Care for Self

Introduction
This could seem like a selfish theme for a Mass! But God definitely cares about us and asks us to take care of ourselves as well.

Scripture says that God is the potter and we are the clay. Each of us is called to make something good of our clay: to care and look after ourselves so that God's life can grow in us.

People care for themselves in different ways: eating the right foods, educating themselves, nurturing the life of friendship, caring for their relationship with God in prayer and the sacraments.

They don't look after themselves when, for example, they drink too much, become lazy, or fail to see themselves as valuable in the sight of God. So, let us pray in this Mass about taking care of ourselves. If we take real care of ourselves, we will likely find ourselves wanting to take care of others.

Penitential Rite
My brothers and sisters, as we prepare to offer Mass together, we ask God's forgiveness for our sins, particularly if we have failed to take care of ourselves.
> Lord Jesus, you grew in knowledge and wisdom in your own life:
> Lord have mercy.
> Lord Jesus, you call us to be with you all the days of our life:
> Christ have mercy.
> Lord Jesus, you are our brother and friend at the right hand of God:
> Lord have mercy.

May almighty God have mercy on us, forgive us our sins, and bring us to everlasting life. Amen.

Opening Prayer
God our Father, you have loved each of us and known each of us
from the first moment of our existence.
You have valued us and rejoiced in us, the people whom you love.
As you care for us, help us to care for ourselves.
As we care for ourselves, help us to care for each other.
We ask this through Jesus Christ, our Lord. Amen.

First Reading *Isaiah 62:2-4*

> *If you hear these words of God in Isaiah, you'll see the value God places on you. Then you know you are worthwhile: it is not selfish to take good care of yourself. The word of God is as true for each of us today as it was when first written.*

A reading from the prophet Isaiah.

You will be called by a new name, one which the mouth of the Lord will confer. You are to be a crown of splendour in the hand of God, a princely diadem in the hand of your God; no longer are you to be named 'Forsaken', nor your land 'Abandoned', but you shall be called 'My delight' and your land 'The Wedded'; for the Lord takes delight in you. As the bridegroom rejoices in his bride, so will your God rejoice in you.

Responsorial Psalm
Psalm 131 A poem of trust in God.
RESPONSE: In you, O Lord, I put my trust.

Lord, my heart has no lofty ambitions,
my eyes do not look too high.
I am not concerned with great things
or marvels beyond my scope. R.

Enough for me to keep my soul quiet and tranquil,
like a child in its mother's arms,
as content as a newborn child. R.

Gospel *Luke 22: 24-27*

> *Jesus values you for who and what you are, not for what you do or what you have achieved. He calls himself the servant; he identifies with the weakest of us. His view of us leads us to care for ourselves.*

A reading from the holy Gospel according to Luke.

An argument also began between them about who should be reckoned the greatest; but he said to them, 'Among the Gentiles it is the kings who lord it over them and those who have authority over them are given the title "Benefactor". With you this must not happen. No; the greatest among you must behave as if he were the youngest, the leader as if he were the one who serves. For who is greater: the one who waits at table or the one who serves? The one at table, surely? Yet here am I among you as one who serves.'

Prayer of the Faithful

Jesus, our brother, help us to see ourselves as you see us: you love us and have given yourself in death for us; Lord, hear us.

Lord, help people who have very little confidence in themselves, especially people who turn to drugs, to find self worth; Lord, hear us.

Help us, Lord, to value people in our society for what they are, not just for what they do; Lord, hear us.

Lord, help us to see the full dignity of everyone, old and young, for we are all children of God; Lord, hear us.

Let us pray:

Gracious God, you have made each person in your own likeness,

and as they mature and develop

you continue to re-create them all their lives.

Give us confidence in your love for us.

We make this prayer through Christ our Lord. Amen.

Preparation of the Gifts

People might bring to the altar 'symbols of care': a book on care of the mind; health food, care of the body; a friendship card, care of the heart; something to symbolize silence and solitude, care of the inner self.

Prayer over the Gifts

We bring to this table, loving God,

the fruits of the earth which you have given us.

You love all you have created.

As we receive the body and blood of Jesus at this table,

help us to know that you love and care for each person.

We ask this through Christ our Lord. Amen.

Communion Reflection

Lord God, writes a poet, 'give my roots rain.'

Take time off each day to think and pray,

to care how your life is going.

Give your roots rain.

Take time with a friend to do nothing too important,

but just to be together, to enjoy another person.

Give your roots rain.

Take time to write a poem or grow a flower,

to create something that is an expression of you.

Give your roots rain.

Take time to play a sport, read a poem, pray a while,
to grow in the different aspects of your life.
Give your roots rain.

For in your roots you find who you are,
and there, too, you find who God is,
for God dwells with you always.

Concluding Prayer
We thank you, God our Father,
for your care for all you have made.
Let us look at everyone through your eyes,
and see each man, woman and child,
as one you care for and love.
We ask this through Christ our Lord. Amen.

21. Jesus Christ

Introduction
Jesus was a man whose influence on people was lasting. And it still is. Our Mass today recalls some of the major goals of his life. In his work for people and in his love, he wanted to see justice, compassion and reconciliation among people. These are three big goals of his people now and of the church. We need them today as the people in his time needed them. He spoke about love in these terms and he lived his message out in his own life. He was concerned about the rights of each person, espec-ially the poor, about forgiveness and reconciliation in a family and a nation, and all the time with compassion, treating each person with dignity. His commitment to his goal in life brought him to death. It was a tough message and a tough life: a life lived to-tally out of love, a love so strong that it is still alive. Let us pray and think about these things at Mass today.

Penitential Rite
Let's pray for forgiveness and healing for sins against the dignity of each person, for ways people are hurt by sins of injustice and violence.
Lord, you forgave those who harmed you:
Lord have mercy.
Lord, you are close to the broken-hearted:
Christ have mercy.
Lord, you are raised from death by the love of the Father:
Lord have mercy.
May almighty God have mercy on us, forgive us our sins, and bring us to everlasting life. Amen.

Opening Prayer
God our Father,
your Son Jesus is our brother and our model.
We see him as one who tried to change what was evil
by giving his life in love of your people.
we pray for gifts like his,
for courage, understanding, and compassion.
We pray in his name, for he is Lord, forever and ever. Amen.

First Reading *1 John 4:16-21*
Jesus is the One who most fully lived the love of God and asks that we

live in the love of God and the love of others. Our reading from the
apostle John links these loves together.

A reading from the first letter of John.

Beloved, let us love one another, because love is from God; everyone who loves is born of God and knows God. Whoever does not love does not know God, for God is love. God's love was revealed among us in this way: God sent his only Son into the world that we might live through him. In this is love, not that we loved God but that God loved us and sent his Son to be the atoning sacrifice for our sins. Beloved, since God loved us so much, we also ought to love one another. No one has ever seen God; if we love one another, God lives in us, and this love is perfected in us.

Responsorial Psalm
Psalm 85 A poem promising the peace and justice of Christ.
RESPONSE: We love others because Christ loved us first.

I will hear what the Lord God has to say,
a voice that speaks of peace,
peace for his people and his friends,
and those who turn to him in their hearts. R.

Mercy and faithfulness have met;
justice and peace have embraced.
Faithfulness shall spring from the earth
and justice look down from heaven. R.

Gospel *John 15:12-17*
Jesus speaks in this gospel of the reason for the way he lived: out of love
for people which brought him to suffering and death.

A reading from the holy Gospel according to John.

Jesus said to his disciples: 'This is my commandment, that you love one another as I have loved you. No one has greater love than this, to lay down one's life for one's friends. You are my friends if you do what I command you. I do not call you servants any longer, because the servant does not know what the master is doing; but I have called you friends, because I have made known to you everything I have heard from my Father. You did not choose me but I chose you. And I appointed you to go and bear fruit, fruit that will last, so that the Father will give you whatever you ask him in my name. I am giving you these commands so that you may love one another.

Prayer of the Faithful

Let's pray at this Mass for people doing the work of Jesus in many ways:

For parents, teachers and all who look after young people; may the Lord help them in their care especially those who look after young people who are ill or depressed in any way, Lord hear us.

For men and women who suffer in their lives in their following of Jesus: who are imprisoned for their commitment to faith and to justice, Lord hear us.

That we may put the concerns and the gospel of Jesus into decisions we make about our careers and hear his call to us, 'Follow me', Lord hear us.

For ourselves: may we be more and more attracted by the goodness of Jesus, and spread this in our lives, Lord hear us.

Lord Christ, you were a man of courage, justice,
compassion and forgiveness.
give us hearts like yours,
so that we may create with you
a world of justice, compassion and forgiveness.
We ask this of the Father in your name. Amen.

Prayer over the Gifts

We pray, gracious God, that we may learn at Mass
what you want of us.
Help us to see all your people as part of your family,
for we are all brothers and sisters in you.
We make this prayer in the name of Christ the Lord. Amen.

Invitation to Communion

This is the Bread of Life, the gift of Jesus in our world today.
We are happy to be called to this Eucharist.
Lord I am not worthy to receive you,
but only say the word and I shall be healed.

Communion Reflection

Above and beyond the words of Jesus
comes the example of his life.
He was born in a stable,
with no influence to get a room in the inn.
He was a citizen of Nazareth,
a bad address,

the kind of place you wouldn't mention
if looking for work.
He was an exile, like millions in our world,
who can't live in their native country
for the same reason as Jesus.
He was a manual worker,
his hands frequently dirty,
often cut,
and a renegade preacher, on the run.
He was finally abandoned by his friends and supporters
and was alone at the mercy of the soldiers.
He was put to death like a criminal slave,
naked on the cross.

adapted from *Peter Lemass*, The Call to be Poor.

Concluding Prayer
Gracious God, by sharing in the bread of life,
we are brought into community with all your people.
We pray that we can be like Jesus your Son,
who lived for others, especially the poor.
may we respect the dignity of all we meet.
Grant this through Christ our Lord. Amen.

22. Courage

Introduction
Many of the most important decisions in our lives involve risk. They involve taking the risk that new relationships, a marriage, a religious commitment, a job, or a course of study, will work out. There's no life without change, and no change without risk. Any time we stick out our necks in support of the poor or the deprived, we risk the scorn of others.

Christianity itself is dangerous . If we really live our convictions, we'll risk being misunderstood by others. Jesus Christ risked a lot. He risked the anger of political leaders and of religious leaders. He risked the misunderstanding of friends, family, and followers.

We risk something because it's worthwhile. That's what we'll pray about at this Mass, and we'll pray, too, for the gift of courage in our lives.

Penitential Rite
We ask now for the courage to do and say what's right in our lives. We ask forgiveness if we have failed to do this and for healing and strength to become men and women of true courage.

Lord Jesus, you came to do your Father's will:
Lord have mercy.
Christ our Lord, you gave your life in service of your people:
Christ have mercy.
Lord Jesus, you have gained the victory over injustice and death:
Lord have mercy.

Opening Prayer
God our Father, give us the gift of courage;
we ask that when we know what is right that we might do it and say it,
remembering Jesus your Son whose life was an example
of courage and trust in you.
Help us to be people who respect
the strength of others' convictions
so that our love and our friendship
and our group-life together
is based on doing and saying what is good in your service.
We ask this through Christ our Lord. Amen.

First Reading *Acts 5:12-21*

> *Consider the risks and courage of the apostles in preaching the message of Jesus. We know of people in different places today suffering similarly for truth, Christ and God.*

A reading from the Acts of the Apostles.

They all used to meet by common consent in the Portico of Solomon. No one else dared to join them, but the people were loud in their praise and the numbers of men and women who came to believe in the Lord increased steadily. So many signs and wonders were worked among the people at the hands of the apostles that people even came crowding in from the towns round about Jerusalem, bringing with them their sick and those tormented by unclean spirits, and all of them were cured.

Then the high priest intervened with all his supporters from the party of the Sadducees. Prompted by jealousy, they arrested the apostles and had them put in the common jail.

But at night the angel of the Lord opened the prison gates, and said as he led them out, 'Go stand in the Temple, and tell the people all about this new Life.' They did as they were told; they went into the Temple at dawn and began to preach.

Responsorial Psalm

Psalm 99 A poem of joy in the service of God.
RESPONSE: Lord, you are with us all our days.

Cry out with joy to the Lord, all the earth.
Serve the Lord with gladness.
Come before him, singing for joy. R.
RESPONSE: Lord, you are with your people all our days.
He made us, we belong to him,
we are his people, the sheep of his flock. R.

Go within his gates, giving thanks.
Enter his courts with songs of praise.
Give thanks to him and bless his name. R.

Gospel

> *This is a story of danger, courage and risk. It's the picture of Peter walking on the water. He is walking toward Jesus and that gives him courage. Our Christian life will often call for risk and courage as we follow what we think God is asking of us.*

A reading from the holy Gospel according to Matthew.

After sending the crowds away, Jesus went up into the hills by himself to pray. When evening came, he was there alone, while the boat, by now far out on the lake, was battling with a heavy sea, for there was a head-wind. In the fourth watch of the night he went towards them, walking on the lake, and when the disciples saw him walking on the lake they were terrified. 'It is a ghost,' they said, and cried out in fear. But at once Jesus called out to them, saying, 'Courage! It is I! Do not be afraid.'

It was Peter who answered. 'Lord,' he said, 'if it is you, tell me to come to you across the water.' 'Come,' said Jesus. Then Peter got out of the boat and started walking toward Jesus across the water, but as soon as he felt the force of the wind, he took fright and began to sink. 'Lord! Save me!' he cried. Jesus put out his hand at once and held him. 'Man of little faith,' he said 'why did you doubt?' And as they got into the boat the wind dropped. The men in the boat bowed down before him and said, 'Truly, you are the Son of God'.

Prayer of the Faithful
We pray now for the gift of courage, for the willingness to take risks in loving others, to care for them and to follow Christ

> For courage to say the things that are truthful and right, and to act upon our convictions, even if others misunderstand:
> *Response: Lord in your goodness, hear our prayer.*

> We pray that our friendship with Jesus will be strong enough to give us courage to do what he wants, that our lives and our relationships be honest and genuine. We know he is ahead of us, calling us into further love and courage: Lord hear us. R.

> For leaders in our state and in our churches, for courage for them to do what is human and right, and that they'll remember the needs of others in their decision-making, especially those who are poor and deprived: Lord hear us. R.

God, our Father, we ask you to be with us in our desires to be courageous in doing what is good. Help us always to see Jesus as one near us, as a companion, and Lord forever and ever. Amen.

Prayer over Gifts
Accept our gifts, Almighty God, we pray,
and give to us the courage of Jesus, your Son,
who has come among us

to offer your love to the poor
and deprived in our world.
We ask this in the name of Christ the Lord. Amen.

Communion Reflection
Courage is like a rock, strong and firm,
not easily yielding to sea or rain;
layer after layer of strength.
Courage is like a hand reaching out
to touch another with hope;
it has fruits of love and of support
that affect the lives of others.
Courage is like Jesus
who compares himself to a rock
and to a tree which bears fruit in plenty.
To be courageous,
standing out in word and deed,
is to share in the life and the goodness of Christ
and in the hope and joy of God.

Concluding Prayer
Bless each person here, loving Father, before we go.
May we always live according to our convictions.
As we gather here in the name of Jesus
may we be strengthened to live in his name, too.
We ask this through Christ our Lord. Amen.

23. Compassion

Introduction

If you have ever experienced compassion you'll know that it's one of the essentials of any good relationship. In the family, in friendship, in love, compassion is the ability to know deeply the joys and troubles of another and to enter into them. You might sometimes ask yourself, 'What's really going on in the people I'm close to, my best friend, father, sister, mother, boyfriend, girlfriend?' We may live close to people and yet be unaware of how they really are.

Compassion is like a key opening a stiff door: it invites you to be yourself and to share yourself, to experience that nobody is alone in the world and that joys and troubles shared are moments of grace and growth. In the Gospel Jesus is compassionate, and he invites each of us, too, to be compassionate. Let us pray for this gift at our Mass today.

Penitential Rite

We ask God's forgiveness for our lack of compassion when we could have been kinder, more generous, and loving. So often we let our own anger or stubbornness deafen us to the pain of another's suffering.
I confess ...

Opening Prayer

We pray for gift of compassion, gracious God.
We ask for the ability to enter
into the feelings of another with love,
and for the generosity to make no judgment on another's life,
even if this tries our patience.
In all this let us experience the joy of knowing
that in compassion we are like you,
the God of compassion.
We ask this through Christ our Lord. Amen.

First Reading *Colossians 3:12-15*

This is a recommendation from Paul to have compassion at the center of our Christian relationships, the ability to share the joys and the sorrows of others. Then he spells out other qualities of compassion.

A reading from the letter of Paul to the Colossians.

You are God's chosen race, his saints; he loves you, and you should be clothed in sincere compassion, in kindness and humility, gentleness and patience. Bear with one another; forgive each other as soon as a quarrel begins. God has forgiven you; now you must do the same. Over all these put on love to keep them together and complete them. And may the peace of Christ reign in your hearts, because it is for this that you were called together as parts of one body.

Responsorial Psalm

Psalm 23 A poem of God's compassion and care.
RESPONSE: The Lord is compassion and love.

The Lord is my shepherd;
there is nothing I shall want.
Fresh and green are the pastures
where he gives me repose.
Near restful waters he leads me,
to revive my drooping spirit. R.

He guides me along the right path;
he is true to his name.
If I should walk in the valley of darkness
no evil would I fear.
You are there with your crook and your staff;
with these you give me comfort. R.

You have prepared a banquet for me
in the sight of my foes.
My head you have anointed with oil;
my cup is overflowing. R.

Surely goodness and kindness shall follow me
all the days of my life.
In the Lord's own house shall I dwell
forever and ever. R.

Gospel *Luke 23:33-34, 39-43*

> *The sign of the Cross is a sign of Jesus' compassion: he could respond to the sufferings of others, even in his own suffering. He was concerned on Calvary for the thieves on either side of him, and for those who were killing him.*

A reading from the holy Gospel according to Luke.

When they reached the place called The Skull, they crucified him there and the two criminals also, one on the right, the other on the left. Jesus said, 'Father, forgive them; they do not know what they are doing.' Then they cast lots to see who would get his clothing.

One of the criminals hanging there abused him. 'Are you not the Christ?' he said. 'Save yourself and us as well.' But the other spoke up and rebuked him, 'Have you no fear of God at all?' he said. We got the same sentence as he did, but in our case we deserved it: we are paying for what we did. But this man has done nothing wrong. Jesus,' he said, 'remember me when you come into your kingdom.' 'Indeed, I promise you,' he replied, 'today you will be with me in paradise.'

Prayer of the Faithful

Let us pray for the ability to be compassionate, and for people we know who offer compassion.

We pray that we can be sensitive to how others find their lives; not judging people just by how they look; knowing that there is so much more going on than meets the eye: Lord hear us.

Response: Lord in your compassion, hear our prayer.

We remember many people who live lonely lives, unheard, neglected: the old, the sick, young people who are shy and insecure, who think they are alone with their problems: Lord hear us. R.

Let's remember people whose lives are poor, hungry, homeless because the hearts of others are cold and unfeeling. We pray to be sensitive to the poverty and misery of others: Lord hear us. R.

We pray, Lord, for all we remember at this Mass. Give all of us hearts that are open to the hopes and troubles of everyone we meet and compassionate toward the faults of others. We pray this through Christ our Lord. Amen.

Prayer over Gifts

We offer to you, great God,
the work of our hands which has gone into making bread and wine;
we offer you, too, the thought and intelligence
which has taught us how to make such food and drink.
We pray that our sharing in this work of human hands
will bring us closer to you, the Creator of all we are and have,
through Jesus Christ our Lord. Amen.

Communion Reflection

If compassion is to be a presence it has to be made manifest by delicate signs: a letter, a phone-call, an understanding look, a discreet gift which says, 'I am with you; I carry it all with you.' Compassion is a hidden and discreet communication which offers hope. The distressed person is in danger of wallowing in despair and in the taste of death. The compassionate friend is there to help another continue on the road, to live this time of mourning or distress with a tiny flame of hope.

Jean Vanier

Concluding Prayer

We have prayed, God our Father, around the table of compassion,
the table of the death and the resurrection of Jesus.
We thank you that we can do this.
We ask that we may take with us to others the fruits and effects
of the death, life, and rising of Jesus your Son,
who is Lord forever and ever. Amen.

24. Trust

Introduction

Our best relationships are based on trust: trusting that what people tell us is true; trusting another's loyalty and friendship; trusting another's commitment, like marriage. We struggle sometimes to trust, not knowing if the other person will be trustworthy enough. We learn about trusting from good times of trust, and also from bad times. Everyone of us has probably had some moments of being let down, at home, in school, at work, with friends. And we feel like never trusting again.

Maybe it's one of the best gifts we can give to each other, the ability to trust, and we can ask ourselves how trustworthy we are. God is someone we can trust; God is faithful. At this Mass we'll pray about trusting, for those who have taught us about trusting, and also that we might learn to trust in God.

Penitential Rite

Let's remember that we need God's help to trust, and often God's healing power to get over experiences of betrayal in the past. We might have let someone down and don't trust ourselves any more, or we've been let down and don't want to trust again.

Lord Jesus, you ask us to trust in the care of God:
Lord have mercy.
Christ our Lord, to trust in the goodness of others is to be like you:
Christ have mercy.
Lord Jesus, you have trusted your Father, even when you were doubtful of his care:
Lord have mercy.

Opening Prayer

God our Father, you are the source of all life, and the source of all love.
You have created and formed each person here
with the loving hand of care and the caring hand of friendship.
We ask you now to strengthen our belief
in the value and worth we each have in your sight.
Help us believe that each of us delights you,
each of us is worth the death of your Son,
Jesus Christ, who is Lord for ever. Amen.

First Reading *Deuteronomy 1:29-32*

> *This Scripture presents God as one who has always been with us, even when we are unaware of it. Our experience of life and our view of God can make this a difficult thing to believe.*

A reading from the book of Deuteronomy.

'And I said to you: Do not take fright, do not be afraid of them. The Lord your God goes in front of you and will be fighting on your side as you saw him fight for you in Egypt. In the wilderness, too, you saw him: how God carried you, as a parent carries a child, all along the road you travelled on the way to this place. But for all this, you put no faith in your God, who had gone in front of you on the journey to find you a camping ground, by night in the fire to light your path, by day in the cloud.'

Responsorial Psalm

Psalm 25 This is a poem of trust in God.

RESPONSE: Teach us to trust in you, our God.

Lord, make me know your ways.
Lord, teach me your paths.
Make me walk in your truth, and teach me:
for you are God my saviour. R.

The Lord is good and upright.
He shows the path to those who stray.
He guides the humble in the right path;
he teaches his way to the poor. R.

Gospel *Luke 18:35-43*

> *This is story about trust. It invites us to trust God and to trust God in each other. A blind man trusted his friends to bring him to Jesus and trusted Jesus to do what was needed. The picture of Jesus in this story is of one who wants to help.*

A reading from the holy Gospel according to Luke.

As Jesus drew near to Jericho there was a blind man sitting at the side of the road begging. When he heard the crowd going past he asked what it was all about, and they told him that Jesus the Nazarene was passing by. So he called out, 'Jesus, Son of David, have pity on me.' The people in front scolded him and told him to keep quiet, but he shouted all the louder. 'Son of David, have pity on me'. Jesus stopped and ordered them to bring the man to him, and when he came up, asked him, 'What do you want me to do for you?' 'Sir', he replied, 'let me see again.' Jesus said to him, 'Receive your sight. Your faith has saved you.' And instantly his sight returned and he followed him praising God, and all the people who saw it gave praise to God for what had happened.

Prayer of the Faithful
We pray for the gift of trust in our lives.

> Let us know that there are many people we can trust, and help us become people whom others can trust: Lord hear us.
> *Response: Lord in your faithfulness, hear our prayer.*
> We remember people who can't trust, who were very hurt in childhood or in friendship; for married people who have been let down: Lord hear us. R.
> Bless everyone who has helped us become people who can trust, parents, friends, family. Help us all enjoy trusting in each other: Lord hear us. R.
> We pray for people who are lonely, depressed, suicidal, because they have nobody they can trust. We hope that our churches can be places where people can meet and help each other: Lord hear us. R.

God our Father, teach us to trust. Give us openness to listen to each other and not to judge; to give the best interpretation to what others say; to feel with them in suffering, pain, and also in joy. We ask this through Christ our Lord. Amen.

Prayer over the Gifts
Lord our God,
you have called us by our name and we can trust in your care.
These signs of bread and wine are gifts
which show your presence.
Help us grow in the ability to trust you and one another.
We ask this through Christ our Lord. Amen.

Invitation to Communion
God cares for us more than for the birds of the air and the flowers of the field, and asks us to share the Bread of the Eucharist.
We are happy to be at this meal.
Lord, I am not worthy to receive you,
but only say the word and I shall be healed.

Communion Reflection

To trust a friend and be trusted
is one of life's fullest experiences.
It is something we need at the depths of our being—
to know we can be open with another and not be let down.
Trusting means letting go of a part of ourselves and not losing it;.
It's like a mother giving a smile or a friend sharing a secret.
Neither is the poorer for it.
Trust grows only where there is willingness
to share ourselves rather than our possessions,
and rejoice in the mystery that we are not all the same
but that each person is a unique creation of God.
Each time we trust we share in the life of God,
who is faithful always, trustworthy through this life
and into an eternity of joy and love.

Concluding Prayer

Gracious God, in the celebration of this Eucharist,
please strengthen our faith,
enliven our hope, and make our love more wholehearted.
We ask these things in the name of Christ the Lord. Amen.

25. Forgiveness

Introduction
We can all feel a sense of guilt before God at times. We may know why—perhaps because of ways we treated others or spoke about them. The Jesus we meet in the Gospel is one who forgives. He knows our weaknesses better than we do.

Sometimes we wonder what exactly sin is. Maybe a good word for it is meanness, like when we know that we have used someone else. This is what turning from God means.

What is often hardest is to forgive ourselves. We remember for a long time ways in which we let others down or used them, cheated or were mean. The forgiveness of God can be a help to us to forgive ourselves. The certainty that God is forgiving can be a healing power for us. That's what we'll pray about in this Mass. We will pray, too, that we can experience deeply in our hearts the forgiveness of God.

Penitential Rite
Lord, we have sinned against you:
Lord have mercy.
Lord, you are kind and compassionate to all who call on you:
Christ have mercy.
Lord, you are our reconciliation with God our Father:
Lord have mercy.

Opening Prayer
We come to you, Father, with confidence.
You understand us, accept us, and forgive us always.
We come with memories of selfishness and sin,
and with broken relationships.
Heal us so that we can be more loving,
that we can forgive others,
and allow your forgiveness to be a strength in our lives.
We ask this in the name of Christ the Lord. Amen.

First Reading *Isaiah 1:16-18*
The reading is about the forgiveness of sins. God's mercy puts the guilt and shame of a person's past where it belongs, in the past.

A reading from the prophet Isaiah.

Take your wrong-doing out of my sight.
Cease to do evil.
Learn to do good, search for justice, help the oppressed,
be just to the orphan, plead for the widow.
Come now, let us talk this over, says the Lord.
Though your sins are like scarlet, they shall be as white as snow;
though they are red as crimson, they shall be like wool.

Responsorial Psalm
Psalm 104 This is a poem celebrating that God always forgives us.
RESPONSE: Lord, you are kind and forgiving.

It is the Lord who forgives all your guilt,
who heals every one of your ills,
who redeems your life from the grave,
who crowns you with love and compassion. R

The Lord is compassion and love,
slow to anger and rich in mercy.
God does not treat us according to our sins
nor repay us according to our faults. R.

As a father has compassion on his children,
the Lord has pity on those who fear him.
As far as the east is from the west,
so far does God remove our sins. R.

Gospel *John 8:1-12*
> *The way Jesus relates to the woman in this story shows the type of for-*
> *giveness God offers: sympathetic, understanding, and accepting of the*
> *person.*

A reading from the holy Gospel according to John.

At daybreak he appeared in the Temple again; and as all the people
came to him, he sat down and began to teach them.

The scribes and Pharisees brought a woman along who had been
caught committing adultery; and making her stand there in full view of
everybody, they said to Jesus, 'Master, this woman was caught in the
very act of committing adultery, and Moses has ordered us in the Law
to condemn women like this to death by stoning. What have you to
say?' They asked him this as a test for something to use against him.
But Jesus bent down and started writing on the ground with his fin-

ger. As they persisted with their question, he looked up and said, 'If
there is one of you who has not sinned, let him be the first to throw a
stone at her.' Then he bent down and wrote on the ground again.
When they heard this they went away one by one, beginning with the
eldest, until Jesus was left alone with the woman, who remained standing there. He looked up and said, 'Woman, where are they? Has no
one condemned you?' 'No one, sir,' she replied. 'Neither do I condemn you,' said Jesus 'go now, and don't sin anymore.'

Prayer of the Faithful
We pray to God for our intentions after hearing this word of forgiveness.

> Let's pray that we may be forgiving of ourselves, knowing that we
> are forgiven by God: Lord hear us.
> *Response: Lord, in your forgiveness, hear our prayer.*
> We pray for anyone who has hurt us, in our family, among our
> friends, or in school; for people who have let us down. Bless them
> and show them your kindness, even when we feel bitter towards
> them: Lord hear us. R.

May your healing power of forgiveness, gracious God,
help us to be tolerant and kind towards ourselves.
May your example of forgiveness, shown in Jesus, help us forgive others.
We pray that your people everywhere may show
in their lives and relationships
the power and strength of forgiveness.
We ask this in the name of Christ the Lord. Amen.

Prayer over the Gifts
Loving God, we pray that through our offering of bread and wine,
and our welcoming of your Son Jesus into our lives,
we may believe more fully in your forgiveness.
Help us to become people of forgiveness in our world,
in the friendship and justice of Jesus,
in whose name we pray. Amen.

Invitation to Communion
This is the bread of God's forgiveness; whoever eats this, receives the
forgiveness of Christ and is called to look with forgiveness on others.
We are happy to be called to this Eucharist.
Lord I am not worthy to receive you,
but only say the word and I shall be healed.

Communion Reflection
To forgive and be forgiven is to enter a world of freedom;
it's to be free of grudges and bitterness
which block and damage love within us
like water hindered in its flow.
It's to be free of misjudgments about others
which can block the growth of friendship
as tangled roots hinder the growth of a tree.
To forgive is to share in the victory of the Cross
from which Jesus forgave those who had harmed him so much.
To forgive is to be strong enough to excuse another and
to give the benefit of the doubt.
To forgive is to grow
into a deeper sharing in the forgiving love of God.

Concluding Prayer
We have received the forgiveness of your Son, God our Father,
and we know you do not hold our past against us.
Help us, through this Eucharist,
to be people who offer to others
the same forgiveness you have given us.
We ask this in the name of Jesus Christ our Lord. Amen.

26. Thanks

Introduction
There is much in life to be thankful for: friends, family, faith, love,
health of the body, talents of the mind, compassion in the heart. We
can be thankful for a purpose in our lives, for a job, for enough money
to live on; for all the people in our lives, young and old. None of us
has everything we want in life, but we can be grateful for all we have.
We are grateful for this group here, for friendship, support, for honesty
and sincerity among us, for times we've needed a friend and found one
here.

Let's be thankful too for our faith; for God who is close to us in love
and forgiveness, and for the support in faith we get from God's people
in the Church.

We're grateful also for ways in which we have become strong through
our difficulties. Friendships that were difficult, or disagreements at
home, or failures in study, have all taught us lessons about life. For this
we are grateful.

Penitential Rite
Lord, you have come to bring joy to the full:
Lord have mercy.
Lord Jesus, you have come to bring us life to the full:
Christ have mercy.
Lord, you are the Resurrection and the Life at the right hand of
God:
Lord have mercy.

Opening Prayer
Loving God, our life is blessed with many good gifts.
Make us truly grateful
for the gifts of our own personalities,
for the people who help us in our lives,
and for courage and strength to overcome our difficulties.
We make this prayer though Christ our Lord. Amen.

First Reading *Philippians 4:4-20*
Here Paul is grateful to God and rejoices in all the circumstances and
the people of his life.

A reading from the letter of Paul to the Philippians.

Rejoice in the Lord always; again I say rejoice. Let your gentleness be known to everyone. The Lord is near. Do not worry about anything but in everything with prayers of thanksgiving let your requests be made known to God. And the peace of God which is beyond all understanding will guard your hearts and your minds in Christ Jesus ....I know what it is to have little, and what it is to have plenty. In any and all circumstances I have learned the secret of being well-fed and of going hungry, of having plenty and of being in need. I can do all things through Jesus Christ who strengthens me. In any case it was kind of you to share my distress. To our God and Father be glory forever and ever. Amen.

Responsorial Psalm
Psalm 110 A poem of thanks to God.
RESPONSE: Great are your good works, loving God.

I will thank the Lord with all my heart
in the meeting of the just and their assembly.
Great are the works of the Lord,
to be pondered by all who love them. R.

God has sent deliverance to his people
and established his friendship forever.
Holy is God's name, to be feared. R.

Gospel *John 21:15-17*
> *The greatest gift of all in life is to love and be loved. That's what Peter realized at the end of Jesus' life; the best gift Jesus had given him was not perfection but the ability to love and be loved in his friendship with Jesus.*

A reading from the holy Gospel according to John.

Jesus said to Simon Peter, 'Simon, son of John, do you love me more than these?' He said to him, 'Yes, Lord, you know that I love you.' Jesus said to him, 'Feed my lambs.' A second time he said to him, 'Simon, son of John, do you love me?' He said to him, 'Yes, Lord, you know I love you'. Jesus said to him, 'Tend my sheep.' He said to him the third time, 'Simon, son of John, do you love me?' Peter felt hurt because he said to him the third time, 'Do you love me?' And he said to him, 'Lord, you know everything; you know that I love you.' Jesus said to him, 'Feed my sheep.'

Prayers of the Faithful

Let's pray that we may be truly grateful for God's gifts and that God may work through us for the good of others.

May the Lord bless all those for whom we are grateful, in our families, our friends and those who help us in any way, Lord hear us.

May the Lord give us hope and optimism in life, and give us a sense of looking on the good side of things, Lord hear us.

We pray for people, especially young people, who find it hard to be grateful, who are depressed and despairing; may they find hope and the friendship of God in their sadness, Lord hear us.

We pray for those people in our families and among our friends who have died; may we be truly grateful for them even in the times of loss and mourning, Lord hear us.

For what has been in our lives, gracious God, we say thanks; for what is to come, we say yes. Make us people of gratitude and hope all the days of our life. We make our prayer through Christ our Lord. Amen.

Presentation of the Gifts

Symbols of joy and thanks might be included in the Presentation of the Gifts: e.g. a picture of a friend, balloons, flowers, thank-you cards, candles, garments, food, etc.

Prayer over the Gifts

Almighty God, we offer you our bread and wine,
and with them we give you thanks
for all that is good in our lives,
especially our faith in Jesus Christ,
for he gives meaning to our lives.
We make this prayer through him. Amen.

Communion Reflection

When we say thanks, we grow a little;
thanks is like food for the heart and soul.

We're thankful for a compliment,
for help with our studies,
for advice in a problem,
for good conversation.
When we're grateful,
we know we depend on others
for most of the good things of life,

and we can't go it alone.

Think for a moment of something you're thankful for
or someone you feel gratitude towards;
allow yourself to feel the thanks in your heart.

Doesn't it make you feel good?
You feel a bit humble,
joyful, excited,
and you feel whole again.

Be grateful this moment
for who you are,
for the friendships in life,
and for the faith you have in God.

Concluding Prayer
Loving God, we go from this place
in thanks for your interest in us.
Make us people who are truly grateful
for the wonders of life,
and for strength and support
in times that are difficult.
We make this prayer through Christ our Lord. Amen.

27. Friendship 1

Introduction
Friendship is something we all need, long for, and hope for. It is what causes the greatest joy in our lives, and can also cause the greatest hurts. In friendship we share secrets with another, develop loyalties that are often intense, and make relationships that sometimes last throughout our lives. Friendship may mean moments of just being together, of shared humour, of discovering the mystery and exciting uniqueness of another person. It's important at all ages; without it life can be lonely, empty, isolated. It's the best gift we can give one to another.

It's also how Jesus describes his relationship with each of us. He says, 'I do not call you servants, I call you friends.' It's a way of experiencing what God is like. When we try to be true friends to each other we have some glimpse of God. In our Mass today we thank God for friends, pray for them, and welcome Jesus into our lives as friend.

Penitential Rite
We call to mind that we are selfish and sinful and that we need God's forgiveness, and the forgiveness of Christ, our friend. We ask for forgiveness especially for ways in which we don't spread friendship.

>Lord Jesus, you call us friends:
>Lord have mercy.
>Christ our Lord, you are a friend of sinners and of everyone:
>Christ have mercy.
>Lord Jesus, you show us God as friend and father:
>Lord have mercy.

Opening Prayer
God our Father, you are the source of all life, and the source of all love.
You have created and formed each person here with the loving hand of care and the caring heart of friendship.
We ask you now to strengthen our belief
in the value and worth we each have in your sight.
Help us believe that each of us delights you,
and that each of us is worth the death of your Son.
We make our prayer through Christ our Lord. Amen.

First Reading *Romans 12:9-18*

> *The ways we recognize Christian friendship are given here by Paul. The list is impressive and the ideal is high. This is a beautiful vision of what friendship is in the heart of Christ.*

A reading from the letter of Paul to the Romans.

Do not let your love be a pretense, but sincerely prefer good to evil. Love each other as much as brothers and sisters should, and have a profound respect for each other. Work for the Lord with untiring effort and with great earnestness of spirit. If you have hope, this will make you cheerful. Do not give up if trials come; and keep on praying. If any of the saints are in need you must share with them; and you should make hospitality your special care.

Bless those who persecute you: never curse them, bless them. Rejoice with those who rejoice and be sad with those in sorrow. Treat everyone with equal kindness; never be condescending but make real friends with the poor. Do not allow yourself to become self-satisfied. Never repay evil with evil but let everyone see that you are interested only in the highest ideals. Do all you can to live at peace with everyone.

Responsorial Psalm

Psalm 91 God's love is forever.

RESPONSE: I do not call you servants, I call you friends.

He who dwells in the shelter of the Most High
and abides in the shade of the Almighty
says to the Lord: 'My refuge,
my stronghold, my God in whom I trust!' R.

His love he set on me, so I will rescue him;
protect him for he knows my name.
When he calls I shall answer: 'I am with you.'
I will save him in distress and give him glory. R.

Gospel *Luke 19:1-10*

> *Notice in this story how Jesus accepts with friendship and understanding a man whom others do not like. An essential quality of friendship is acceptance of the other person.*

A reading from the holy Gospel according to Luke.

Jesus entered Jericho and was going through the town when a man whose name was Zacchaeus made his appearance; he was one of the senior tax collectors and was a wealthy man. He was anxious to see what kind of man Jesus was, but he was too short and could not see him for the crowd; so he ran ahead and climbed a sycamore tree to catch a glimpse of Jesus who was to pass that way. When Jesus reached the spot he looked up and spoke to him: 'Zacchaeus, come down. Hurry, because I must stay at your house today.' And he hurried down and welcomed him joyfully. They all complained when they saw what was happening. 'He has gone to stay at a sinner's house,' they said. But Zacchaeus stood his ground and said to the Lord, 'Look, sir, I am going to give half my property to the poor, and if I have cheated any-body I will pay them back four times the amount.' And Jesus said to him, 'Today salvation has come to this house because this man ,too, is a son of Abraham; for the Son of Man has come to seek out and save what was lost.'

Prayer of the Faithful

We pray now to God about the gift of friendship. We remember peo-ple we'd like to pray for.

For our friends, we ask you to bless them, especially any of them who are in trouble: Lord hear us.

Response: Lord in your friendship, hear our prayer.

We ask that we'll always value the gift of friendship, that we don't do anything through gossip or lies to ruin it for others or for our-selves: Lord hear us. R.

For those who find it hard to make friends because of shyness or in-security or embarrassment, or because of problems at home, make us sensitive to them and offer friendship to them: Lord hear us. R.

For friendship between nations, for peace and justice in our own countries, and that developed countries may not abuse the poverty of other nations: Lord hear us. R.

God our Father, increase in us the desire to make friends, both to be a friend and to receive friendship. Thank you for this gift, and for giving yourself to us as a friend. We pray through Christ our Lord. Amen.

Prayer Over the Gifts

We offer to you God, Creator and Friend,
all the good desires of our lives;
we want to be people who can love as you love,
who can see in each of us here
a reflection of yourself and your love,
as bread and wine are a reflection, for you and for us,
of the death and love of Jesus your Son,

who is Lord forever and ever. Amen.

Invitation to Communion

This is the Lamb of God, Jesus who calls us friend, who says to each
person here, 'Today I am going to come to your house.'
We are happy to be called to this Eucharist.
Lord, I am not worthy to receive you,
but only say the word and I shall be healed.

Communion Reflection

Guests of my life
You came in the early dawn, and you came in the night.
Your name was uttered by the spring flowers
and yours by the shower of rain.
You brought the harp into my life and you brought the lamp.
After you had taken your leave
I found God's footprints on the floor.
Now when I am at the end of my pilgrimage
I leave in the evening flowers of worship my salutations to you all.

Tagore

Concluding Prayer

Gracious God, in the celebration of this Eucharist
you strengthen our faith,
enliven our hope, and make our love more wholehearted.
We go from here with the joy and the courage
of your companionship all the days of our lives.
And we thank you in the name of Christ the Lord. Amen.

28. Friendship 2

Introduction

In this Mass we thank God for the friends we have, and we pray for them. Friendship is something all of us want, and all of us look for. In friendship we share our lives with another; we are there in good times and bad. We can help another in trouble, and share successes and joy.

Life without friends is a lonely life, and many find it that way. We need to care for our friends, to give them time by being together with them, to talk together, have fun. Friendship doesn't come automatically. It grows with time spent together, with forgiveness after arguments and misunderstandings. It grows also in the trust that we are accepted by another.

God is the source of friendship, and when we have found a friend, we share in the life of God. At this Mass let's pray that all of us can grow in our capacity to be friends, now and in the future.

Penitential Rite

The Mass is the love of God made visible in Jesus Christ, who calls us his friends. Let us ask God's forgiveness for our sins.

You call us friends because you have made yourself known to us:
Lord have mercy.
You are Son of God and friend of everyone:
Christ have mercy.
You are with God, our friend, in the kingdom of heaven:
Lord have mercy.

May almighty God have mercy on us, forgive us our sins, and bring us to life everlasting. Amen.

Opening Prayer

Loving God, you are the source of all friendship.
Help us to be good friends to each other;
help us also to offer friendship, when we can,
to those who are lonely or in need.
We make this prayer through Christ our Lord. Amen.

First Reading 1 Corinthians 13:4-8

The qualities of love in this letter of Paul are the qualities of a good friendship.

A reading from the first letter of Paul to the Corinthians.

Love is always patient and kind; it is never jealous;
love is never boastful or conceited; it is never rude or selfish;
it does not take offense, and is not resentful.
Love takes no pleasure in other people's sins,
but delights in the truth;
it is always ready to excuse,
to trust, to hope, and to endure whatever comes.

Responsorial Psalm

Psalm 139 God is a true friend who knows us through and through.
RESPONSE: We thank you for the wonder of friendship.

Lord, you search me and you know me,
you know my resting and my rising,
you discern my purpose from afar. R.

For it was you who created my being,
knit me together in my mother's womb,
I thank you for the wonder of my being,
for the wonders of all your creation. R.

Gospel *John 15:12-17*

Friendship is how Jesus looks on his relationship with his disciples, and this is how he thinks of each of us, too.

A reading from the holy Gospel according to John.

One can have no greater love than to lay down one's life for one's friends. You are my friends if you do what I command you. I shall not call you servants any more, because a servant does not know the master's business; I call you friends, because I have made known to you everything I have learned from my Father. What I command you is to love one another.

Prayer of the Faithful

Let us now make our intentions to God, who calls us friends:
We pray for our friends; may you bless them and give them happiness; Lord, hear us.
We pray that we can be open to making friends with many kinds of people, realizing that everyone needs friends; Lord, hear us.
We pray for people who find it difficult to make friends, who find it difficult to trust or to be honest with people; Lord, hear us.

For those who are lonely, especially young people who find themselves turning to drink, drugs, or superficial relationships to give
themselves a sense of meaning in their lives; Lord, hear us.

For everyone who has shown love to us in our lives; Lord, hear us.

Let us pray:

Gracious God, from you comes every good gift,
and we thank you for the gift of friendship.
Help us to learn to be people who can trust,
be honest and be faithful in our friendships.
We ask this through Christ our Lord. Amen.

Presentation of the Gifts
Symbols of friendship might be placed on the altar at the Preparation of
the Gifts: *a letter, a ring, a candle, or other symbols that would suggest
friendship to the group.*

Prayer over the Gifts
Loving God, friend of your people,
friend of the world, friend of the earth:
be with us as we journey together in life to you.
May this bread and wine
always remind us of your friendship
in Jesus Christ our Lord. Amen.

Communion Reflection
I think of people I met in the past.
A friend in primary school: we used to hang around together;
a girl in high school when I first fell in love;
a university friend who shared the same courses.
Many, many people. Where are they now?
Some are still friends, others just send a Christmas card;
Many I no longer meet, but I have never forgotten them.
Not every friendship lasts forever;
we move away, change schools or jobs,
and we drift away from one another,
but every memory of friendship shared, even for a short time,
is a treasure, like sunshine and warmth in our lives,
like a cool breeze on a humid day,
like a shower of rain refreshing the earth.
Thank you, loving God
for the gift of friendship at every time of life.

Concluding Prayer

God our Father, in Jesus you give us your own friendship.

We thank you for this gift.

Help us to cherish it and nourish it,

and never demean it for anyone.

Make us true friends

in the name and the spirit of Christ our Lord. Amen.

29. Family

Introduction

Our family life is one of the most important and significant areas of our lives. It can bring great happiness or unhappiness to us and this Mass is a time to pray for our families. We're thankful for the care and love we get in our families. At times, we don't always experience that love and care, so we also pray for those families who are having difficulties.

We learn a lot about life in our families: the first people we love and quarrel with are in the family. We learn how to get along with others, how to deal with frustrations, how to give and take in day to day life.

No family is completely happy; each has its problems. But the family is our beginning, our rock, our security. We move away from it as we get older, but the family is the place to which we can come back for love and support.

Jesus grew up in a family with Mary and Joseph and an extended family of cousins, aunts, and uncles, who must have played a large role in his life. In this Mass let us pray for our parents and brothers and sisters, that each of us will contribute to the happiness of our own family life.

Penitential Rite

As we begin our Mass, we ask God's forgiveness for sin, especially for being selfish at home and for hurting our parents, sisters, and brothers.
Lord Jesus, you are Son of God and son of Mary:
Lord have mercy.
Lord Jesus, you are word made flesh:
Christ have mercy.
Lord Jesus, you are our brother at the right hand of God:
Lord have mercy.

Opening Prayer

God our Father, creator of all who live,
you sent your Son among us
to gather us together as brothers and sisters.
He grew up in a family with Mary and Joseph, and so
we ask his help in our family life.

May we know contentment, peace, and happiness in our homes
We ask this through Christ our Lord. Amen.

First Reading *Colossians 3:12-15,17*
   This is an ideal of the qualities of family life.

A reading from the letter of Paul to the Colossians.

As the chosen of God, then, the holy people whom God loves, you are
to be clothed in heartfelt compassion, in generosity and humility, gentleness and patience. Bear with one another; forgive each other if one
of you has a complaint against another. The Lord has forgiven you;
now you must do the same. Over all these, put on love, the perfect
bond. And may the peace of Christ reign in your hearts, because it is
for this that you were called together in one body. Always be thankful.
Whatever you say or do, let it be in the name of the Lord Jesus, in
thanksgiving to God the Father through him.

Responsorial Psalm
Psalm 127 A poem of God's care us always.
RESPONSE: God provides for all his family.

If the Lord does not build the house,
in vain do the builders labour;
if the Lord does not watch over the city,
in vain does the watchman keep vigil. R.

Truly children are a gift from God,
a blessing, the fruit of the womb.
Indeed the children of youth
are like arrows in the hand of a warrior. R.

Gospel *Luke 1:39-45*
   *In the simplicity of a family scene with Mary and Elizabeth, both ex-
   pecting a child, God visits us. It is in our families that we first hear of
   God and we first experience love and care.*

A reading from the holy Gospel according to Luke.

Mary set out at that time and went as quickly as she could to a town in
the hill country of Judaea. She went into Zechariah's house and greet-
ed Elizabeth. Now as soon as Elizabeth heard Mary's greeting, the
child leapt in her womb and Elizabeth was filled with the Holy Spirit.
She gave a loud cry and said, 'Of all women, you are the most blessed

and blessed is the fruit of your womb. Why should I be honoured with a visit from the mother of my Lord? The moment your greeting reached my ears, the child in my womb leapt for joy. Yes, blessed is she who believed that God's promise would be fulfilled.'

Prayer of the Faithful
Let us make our intentions to God now, praying especially for our families and for the good of family life:
> We pray for our parents, living and dead; may God reward them always for all they do and have done for us; Lord, hear us.
> We pray for our sisters and brothers; may we grow to love and understand each other in our family life and overcome our differences and quarrels; Lord, hear us.
> For any families we know who are struggling with sickness or unemployment; Lord, hear us.
> For those families suffering through bad relationships and for those who are separated we ask for God's healing power; Lord, hear us.

Let us pray:
May family love, peace, and contentment grow, loving God, and may we learn to understand each other's difficulties and strains.
Give us the grace of forgiveness and tolerance for each other.
We ask this through Christ our Lord. Amen.

Presentation of the Gifts
Bring up symbols of family life: a photo album, a key, a picture of grandparents, anything that reminds the group of family.

Prayer over the Gifts
We give to you, gracious God, these small gifts of bread and wine.
They are our invitation to you to be part of our family life,
for they are signs of your love for us.
May we who offer these gifts offer also our service to you.
Grant this through Christ our Lord. Amen.

Communion Reflection
Jesus knew the joys and sorrows of family life.
Living for many years with Mary and Joseph,
he learned the joy of closeness with parents,
the joy of getting to know them
and the joy of their love.
He knew, too, the sorrow of death when Joseph died,

and that his parents experienced hardship because of him,
forced as they were out of their homeland when he was born.
They felt sorrow again when he was lost in Jerusalem,
and Mary saw him suffering and dying on a cross.
He left home, knowing his mission in life,
and Mary, the mother who loved him,
had to learn to let him go.
She had to learn to be his mother in a new way, and in so doing,
she became our mother, too.
The Word became one of us,
fully one of us, the son of a family;
the Son of God shared our family life.

Concluding Prayer
As we go from this place, loving God,
where we have celebrated the love of Jesus your Son,
we ask you to bless us and all our family members.
May all we do and say be words and deeds
that Jesus would see as his.
Grant this through Christ our Lord. Amen.

30. Vocation 1

Introduction

We've all met people who have answered a call from God in their lives. Each of us, by our baptism, is called to follow Christ and his Gospel. It's our free choice to say yes or no to that calling.

We may spend a while wondering how to answer that call: through marriage, religious life, single life, or priesthood. Or in what work will we be able to imitate Jesus and spread his love, peace, and justice in our world?

Our Mass today reflects on this aspect of our relationship with God: the call to serve Christ in whatever way we can. Let's pray about that now.

Penitential Rite

We pray for God's forgiveness for ways in which we and all peoples fail to answer the Gospel call to kindness and compassion, to love and service in our world.

You have come to call sinners to repentance:
Lord have mercy.
You have come to call not the holy but sinners:
Christ have mercy.
You have overcome sin and you offer forgiveness to all your people:
Lord have mercy.

Opening Prayer

God our Father, you have called us
through our family and through baptism
to hear your word and be followers of Jesus your Son.
We sometimes fear what you might ask of us.
Help us to know that, in any way we try to respond to your call,
you will be with us, never asking more than we can give.
We are joyful that you do call us,
and are helped by each other's faith and response to your call.
Give us enthusiasm and joy in your service.
We ask this through Christ our Lord. Amen.

First Reading *Jeremiah 1:4-10*

This is an account of a call in the bible: Jeremiah is called by God. He knows his own weakness and resists the call, but God promises help.

A reading from the prophet Jeremiah.

The Lord said to me, 'I chose you before I gave you life, and before you were born I selected you to be a prophet to the nations.' I answered, 'Sovereign Lord, I don't know how to speak; I am too young.'

But the Lord said to me, 'Do not say that you are too young, but go to the people I send you to, and tell them everything I command you to say. Do not be afraid of them, for I will be with you to protect you. I, the Lord, have spoken!'

Then the Lord stretched out his hand, touched my lips, and said to me, 'Listen, I am giving you the words you must speak. Today I give you authority over nations and kingdoms to uproot and pull down, to destroy and to overthrow, to build and to plant.'

Responsorial Psalm
Psalm 36 This psalm is a prayer to do the will of God.
RESPONSE: Come, follow me, says the Lord.

How many, O Lord my God,
are the wonders and designs
that you have worked for us;
you have no equal.
Should I proclaim and speak of them,
they are more than I can tell! R.

You do not ask for sacrifice and offerings,
but an open ear.
You do not ask for holocaust and victim.
here am I. R.

In the scroll of the book it stands written
that I should do your will.
My God, I delight in your law
in the depth of my heart. R.

Gospel *John 20:19-21*
We hear the words of the risen Lord about being sent. That is what vocation entails: God sends us into partnership with Jesus to spread the gospel in whatever way we can.

A reading from the holy Gospel according to John.

It was late that Sunday evening, and the disciples were gathered together behind locked doors, because they were afraid of the Jewish authorities. Then Jesus came and stood among them. 'Peace be with you,' he said. After saying this, he showed them his hands and his side. The disciples were filled with joy at seeing the Lord. Jesus said to them again, 'Peace be with you. As the Father sent me, so I send you.'

Prayer of the Faithful
We pray now for people who are following, in various ways, the call of God in their lives, and for ourselves that we might also respond to God.

For married people, especially our own parents, who are trying to bring up their children in the spirit of love: Lord hear us.
Response: Lord, in your friendship, hear our prayer.
For priests and religious, especially those in situations where they are helping in the struggle for justice and peace: Lord hear us. R.
For all of us here, we pray that we can give the Gospel of Christ a central place in making our life-decisions: Lord hear us. R.

Let us pray:
God our Father, help us to believe
that you are constantly calling us into the friendship of Jesus and that our friendship is shown in kindness and service of your people.
We ask this through Christ the Lord. Amen.

Prayer over the Gifts
Gracious God, take our bread and wine
which are signs not just of our service
but of the loving service of Christ in our world.
We join our work with his for the praise of your name,
and he is Lord forever and ever. Amen.

Invitation to Communion
Jesus was asked, 'Where do you live?' He lives in bread and wine, because these are ordinary signs of his people's lives. We are happy that he says to us, 'Come and see' and happy to be called to this Eucharist.
Lord I am not worthy to receive you,
but only say the word and I shall be healed

Communion Reflection
'What can I do?'
Respect that question.

Trust that you, one man, one woman,
can do for God what otherwise would not be done.
Trust that some people will hear the gospel of Jesus,
that some who are in need will find the touch of human love,
that others will find a listening ear or a voice in their poverty,
only because you have chosen to give God
a central place in your life ...
It is not just your work, your choice, your decision.
You choose because you are chosen,
you choose because in the heart of your desire to love,
you have found the heart of God searching for you.

Come, Follow Me (Pastoral of the Irish Bishops, 1989)

Concluding Prayer
We have gathered here around this table,
Loving God, to hear your word
and to receive the bread of life, the bread of hope.
We hear your words of calling,
invitation and challenge.
May this Eucharist bring us closer to Jesus,
the one through whom you call us.
We ask this through Christ our Lord. Amen.

31. Vocation 2

This Mass is especially suitable for a retreat weekend that focuses on vocation.

Introduction

Our prayer at Mass today is for light and clarity, now or in the future, about our vocation. Each of us must ask ourselves what God is calling us to do with our lives. We want to live for God and others and we trust that whatever way God calls us is what is best for us. God looks into our hearts, knows us, and invites us to a way of discipleship that will bring out the best in us.

We are here then to think, to pray and to talk together about our life questions; we are here to ask to know God's will in our lives. In our Mass we hear the word of God and pray for each other: for light to know what God is asking of each of us, courage to follow it, and trust to believe that this way will bring joy in our own lives and to people we meet and work for in the future.

Penitential Rite

As we prepare to celebrate the mystery of God's love in our lives, we ask forgiveness for our sins and our selfishness:
> You have called us from death into life:
> Lord have mercy.
> You have called us from darkness into your own light:
> Christ have mercy.
> You are pleading for us at the right hand of the Father:
> Lord have mercy.

May almighty God have mercy on us, forgive us our sins, and bring us to life everlasting. Amen.

Opening Prayer

God our Father,
you have been with us
on our way to this point of decision in our lives.
Give us light to know what your call in our lives is
and courage to do what you ask.
We make this prayer through Christ our Lord. Amen.

First Reading *Philippians 3:7-14*

> *Paul writes here of his one desire in life: to know Jesus Christ in his death and resurrection, and to spend his life in companionship with*

him. This is the true meaning of a Christian vocation.

A reading from the letter of Paul to the Philippians.

Because of Christ I have come to consider all advantages that I had as disadvantages. Not only that, but I believe nothing can happen that will outweigh the supreme advantage of knowing Christ Jesus, my Lord. For him I have accepted the loss of everything, and I look on everything as so much rubbish if only I can have Christ, and be given a place in him. I am no longer trying for perfection by my own efforts, the perfection that comes from the Law, but I want only the perfection which comes through faith in Christ, and is from God and based on faith. All I want is to know Christ and the power of his resurrection and to share his sufferings by reproducing the pattern of his death. That is the way I can hope to take my place in the resurrection of the dead. Not that I have become perfect yet: I have not yet won, but I am still running, trying to capture the prize for which Christ Jesus captured me. I can assure you I am far from thinking I have already won. All I can say is that I forget the past and I strain ahead for what is still to come. I am racing for the finish, the prize to which God calls us upwards to receive in Christ Jesus.

Responsorial Psalm
Psalm 27 A poem of trust in the Lord and a request to know his way.
RESPONSE: Show us your pathway, Lord God, for our lives.

The Lord is my light and my help;
whom shall I fear?
The Lord is the stronghold of my life;
before whom shall I shrink? R.

Do not abandon or forsake me,
O God my help!
Instruct me, Lord, in your way,
on an even path lead me. R.

Gospel *Mark 10:41-45*
The call of Jesus is a call to service. This comes out in the story from Mark's gospel where Jesus compares his work in the world with the work of the 'famous': his is the way of service.

A reading from the holy Gospel according to Mark.

When the other ten heard this they began to feel indignant with James and John, so Jesus called them to him and said to them, 'You know that among the pagans their so-called rulers lord it over them, and their great ones make their authority felt. This is not to happen among you. No, anyone who wants to become great among you must be your servant, and anyone who wants to be first among you must be slave to all. For the Son of Man himself did not come to be served but to serve, and to give his life as a ransom for many.'

Prayer of the Faithful

Let us pray to God for our intentions as we gather together in the name of Jesus the Lord:

Give us clarity to know your will in our lives, courage to do what we know is your will, and always a deep love of you and of your people; Lord, hear us.

Give us joy always in doing what is right in our lives; help us to know you as the God of life and of joy; Lord, hear us.

We pray for priests and religious, married couples, and single people everywhere: especially for those working for peace and justice; Lord, hear us.

For all who have helped us in our life of faith, for our parents, family and friends, may the Lord bless them; Lord, hear us.

Let us pray:

God our Father, you have called us into your service.
Give us joy and delight in knowing you and loving you;
give us courage to do what is best for each of us.
We ask this through Christ our Lord. Amen.

Prayer over the Gifts

Gracious God, your Son offered himself on the Cross
for love of your people.
May we share in his risen work
of inviting others into your love.
Make us men and women of strong faith in your service.
We ask this through Christ our Lord. Amen.

Communion Reflection

God's call brings out the best in each person.
A young man or woman who follows God's call
will grow in openness and humanity.
The call of Jesus is for life and life more abundant.
Do you find a leap of joy in thinking of priesthood,

an excitement of giving your life as a religious,
a sense of peace about marriage and family life?
Like the sunrise after the darkness,
or the sunshine after rain,
or the reconciliation after bitterness,
following God's call brings real joy, change, and newness.
It is felt in the joy of the heart,
and in the desire to be like Jesus, the Christ in the world.
It's felt also in deep trust:
God's faithfulness is like the lighthouse in the fog,
like the support of a friend in times that are tough,
like the touch of a hand in the dark.
May we all have the courage
to follow what is best and right in own lives,
and joy in knowing that real life is life in God's company.
Amen.

Concluding Prayer
God our Father,
as we go from this table strengthened
and nourished by the bread of life,
help us to be this bread of life among your people.
We make this prayer through Christ our Lord. Amen.

32. Care for the Earth 1

Introduction

We can look at creation in different ways. Some people use the earth's resources for good, others for selfish purposes. We can be horrified at the way forests have been cleared to make huge profits for industry, thus resulting in floods and starvation. Or how water and air have been polluted.

The earth has been given to us by God to be cared for, treasured, enjoyed, used for the benefit of all. Jesus was a lover of the earth in how he spoke of it, and he saw the finger of God in all of creation.

At Mass today, we give thanks for the earth. We pray for God's forgiveness for the way we misuse it, and we pray that we may be truly grateful for it and treat it well.

Penitential Rite

We ask God's mercy and pardon in our lives, particularly for ways in which we misuse the earth.

God of the earth,
God of the fire,
God of the fresh waters,
God of the shining stars:
Heavenly Father, have mercy on us.

God who made the world,
God of the many tongues,
God of the nations,
God of golden goodness:
Heavenly Father, have mercy on us.

(from the Irish)

Opening Prayer

God our Creator,
you created everything and you saw that it is good.
Help us to care for what you have made,
for the earth, for our rivers, for our beaches,
for all the resources of the earth,
and to use them that people may live in dignity and in safety.
We ask this through Christ our Lord. Amen.

First Reading *Colossians 1:15-18*

> *Everything created is created in Jesus Christ; all of our world can re-*
> *mind us of him. This song of praise is about that. If we sing in joy for*
> *all creation, how could we not but treat it well?*

A reading from the letter of Paul to the Colossians.

He is the image of the unseen God,
the firstborn of all creation,
for in him were created all things
in heaven and on earth:
everything visible and everything invisible,
all things were created through him and for him.
He exists before all things
and in him all things hold together,
and he is the head of the body,
that is, the Church.

Responsorial Psalm

Psalm 8 A poem of praise and joy for all God's creation.
RESPONSE: How great is your name, O Lord, our God,
through all the earth.

When I see the heavens, the work of your hands,
the moon and the stars which you arranged,
what are we that you should keep us in mind,
or your children that you care for us? R.

Yet you have made us little less than gods,
with glory and honour you crown us,
give us power over the work of your hands,
put all things under our feet. R.

All of the sheep and cattle,
yes, even the savage beasts,
birds of the air and fish
that make their way through the waters. R.

Gospel *Matthew 6:25-34*

> *Jesus looks at God's creation and is full of thanks. He asks his disciples*
> *to look at all that God has made and cares for, and see that God cares*
> *even more for them.*

A reading from the holy Gospel according to Matthew.

I am telling you not to worry about your life and what you are to eat, nor about your body and what you are to wear. Surely life is more than food and the body more than clothing! Look at the birds in the sky. They do not sow or reap or gather into barns, yet your heavenly Father feeds them. Are you not worth much more than they are? Do not worry; do not say, 'What are we to eat? What are we to drink? What are we to wear?' Set your hearts on God's kingdom first, and on God's saving justice, and all these other things will be given you as well.

Prayer of the Faithful

Let us pray to the Lord who loves all created things.

Be with all those who care for your creation: people who work for the preservation of the environment, people who give time to keeping the world beautiful; Lord, hear us.

Give us the sensitivity to work so that everyone has an equal share of the world's resources, especially space for a home and food for the table; Lord, hear us.

Help us to see your beauty in the beauty of the world;
Lord, hear us.

Help us to take action against the damage done to creation, the pollution of our seas and forests, and all other sorts of damage to the environment; Lord, hear us.

Let us pray: Lord, you are the creator of all in the world,
and you hate nothing of what you create.
Give us a love for your world,
give us a sense that we are to care for this world.
We ask this through Christ our Lord. Amen.

Presentation of the Gifts

Symbols of creation could be brought to the altar, and, in silence, placed with the bread and wine. Or, alternatively, put a small mound of earth in the sanctuary with plants, fruit, water, and other symbols of creation in it. Put there also the bread and wine and let them be taken from there to the altar while saying the Prayer over the Gifts.

Prayer over the Gifts

Gracious God, from the many gifts you give us,
we place this bread and wine on your altar.
We know that many people badly need ordinary food and drink.
Make us caring people like your Son, Jesus Christ our Lord. Amen.

Communion Reflection

Be open to this mysterious and obscure sense of presence.
God is there: in the mountains and the ocean,
in the flowers and the birds, in the trees and the fields.
Walk through green fields or the brown bog,
walk beside the ocean, listening to every sound,
aware of the beauty and, above all,
conscious of the enveloping presence
that hovers over everything.
This can be exhilarating prayer.
For God is wonderfully present in all things,
working in all things, giving to us in all things.
We cannot see or touch God;
but we can sometimes sense God's healing presence.
When your mind and heart are troubled,
walk and look at nature.
Feel the air and the rain washing your body and cleansing your spirit.
Eat and drink copiously
from the energizing, liberating, healing, life-giving table of life.

William Johnston SJ, *Being In Love.*

Concluding Prayer

As we go from this table of your word
and the communion of your love,
may we bring with us, loving God,
an appreciation of the beauty of all you make,
and a strong faith in the unique beauty of each person
who is made in your image and likeness.
We ask this through Christ our Lord. Amen.

33. Care for the Earth 2

Introduction

We can look at creation in different ways. Some people use the earth's resources for good, others for selfish purposes. We can be horrified at the way forests have been cleared to make huge profits for industry, resulting in floods and starvation. Or how water and air have been polluted.

The earth has been given to us by God to be cared for, treasured, enjoyed, used for the benefit of all. At Mass today, we give thanks for the earth. We pray for God's forgiveness for the way we misuse it, and we pray also that we may be truly grateful for it and treat it well.

Penitential Rite

As we celebrate the love of God in Jesus Christ, let us ask God's forgiveness for our sins and sinfulness.

Lord you have given us the wonders of the world for the enjoyment of your people:
Lord have mercy.
You have asked us to use well the resources of the earth:
Christ have mercy.
You are the Son of God who walked and loved our earth:
Lord have mercy.

May Almighty God have mercy on us, forgive us our sins, and bring us to life everlasting. Amen.

Opening Prayer

God our Father, we thank you for the earth.
Give us love for all you have created;
love for the earth, love for the sea, love for our cities.
Give us, above all, love for your people, created in your own image.
We ask this through Christ our Lord. Amen.

First Reading *Ecclesiasticus 43:13*

This is a song of praise to God for all creation. When we praise God for the earth and the whole world, we can ask ourselves how we use created things.

A reading from the book of Ecclesiasticus.

Praise the Lord, my soul,
Lord my God, how great you are!
Clothed in majesty and splendour,
wearing the light as a robe.

You fixed the earth on its foundations;
in the ravines you opened up springs,
running down between the mountains;
from your high halls you water the mountains,
satisfying the earth with the fruit of your works:

for cattle you make the grass grow,
and for people the plants they need,
to bring forth food from the earth,
food to make them sturdy of heart.

How countless are your works, O Lord,
all of them made so wisely.

Responsorial Psalm
Psalm 8 A poem of praise for God's creation.
RESPONSE: How great is your name, O Lord, our God,
through all the earth.

When I see the heavens, the work of your hands,
the moon and the stars which you arranged,
what are we that you should keep us in mind,
or your children that your care for us? R.

Yet you have made us little less than gods,
with glory and honour you crown us,
give us power over the work of your hands,
put all things under our feet. R.

All of the sheep and cattle,
yes, even the savage beasts,
birds of the air and fish
that make their way through the waters. R.

Gospel *Matthew 14:13-21*
> *Jesus uses food, one of God's greatest created gifts, as a way of showing the generosity and love of God. As we hear this gospel we are reminded that the food of the earth is for everyone. And then we wonder why so many are starving.*

A reading from the holy Gospel according to Matthew.

When evening came, the disciples went to him and said, 'This is a lonely place, and time has slipped by; so send the people away, and they can go to the villages to buy themselves some food.' Jesus replied, 'There is no need for them to go: give them something to eat yourselves.' But they answered, 'All we have with us is five loaves and two fish.' So he said, 'Bring them to me.' He gave orders that the people were to sit down on the grass; then he took the five loaves and the two fish, raised his eyes to heaven and said the blessing. And breaking the loaves he handed them to his disciples, who gave them to the crowds. They all ate as much as they wanted, and they collected the scraps left over, twelve baskets full.

Prayer of the Faithful
As we pray this Mass, let us make our intentions known to God:
> We pray for people all over the world who are hungry; help us to use all the resources of the world to feed them; Lord, hear us.
> We pray for all who are sick, especially children; help us to use all our medical resources for the benefit of all God's people; Lord, hear us.
> We pray for people who have no homes; we pray that the space of the world be equally shared so that all have shelter; Lord, hear us.
> We pray for all who work against nuclear disaster; instead of weapons of destruction, may the world come to see the sense of spending resources so that people may live in dignity and peace; Lord, hear us.

Let us pray:
God our Father, give food to the hungry, heal the sick,
make your home among your people.
Give us the power to work for a world
that shares its resources more justly with all people.
Grant this through Christ our Lord. Amen.

Presentation of the Gifts
Symbols of creation might be brought to the altar, and in silence placed with the bread and wine.

Prayer over the Gifts
Gracious God, from the many gifts you give us,
we place this bread and wine on your altar.

We know that many people badly need ordinary food and drink
as all of us need the food and drink
which you give us in this sacrament.
Make us like your Son, Jesus Christ our Lord, Amen.

Communion Reflection

'There lives the dearest freshness deepdown things.'
What would come to mind?
A daffodil blowing in the wind?
A feather caught in the gate of a sheepfold?
Earth, damp and strong?
And you feel you're part of all God's creation
and all is very good.
A joy to believe in God the Creator,
a joy to partake in creation:
a child's first smile,
an old man's gentle hardworked hand,
the air you breathe,
the water that refreshes:

The peace of God,
the life of Christ,
the joy of the Spirit.

'There lives the dearest freshness deepdown things'.
What else might come to mind?
The smog that darkens a city,
the river polluted and fish killed,
the burns of war on a child's back,
the young man or girl near the bomb at the wrong time,
the garden vandalized just for the hell of it?

And you dread being part of all that,
part of the destruction of what God has planned,
all that is very good is for our stewarding.

Father, forgive the violence that shatters your peace;
Jesus, forgive our neglect of life,
Spirit, forgive the destruction of beauty that we cause.

Father, thank you for the peace of your creation,
Jesus, thank you for the life you bring,
Spirit, thank you for the beauty of your life.

Concluding Prayer

As we go from this table of your word
and the communion of your love,
may we bring with us, Lord God,
an appreciation of the beauty of all you make,
and a strong faith in the unique beauty
of each person who is made in your image and likeness.
We ask this through Christ our Lord. Amen.

34. The Third World 1

Introduction
In this Mass we're going to pray for people in the third world, and for people who are working there to better conditions. We've all seen pictures on TV and in the papers of hunger, starvation, homelessness, and the utter misery of millions of people.

These are children of God, brothers and sisters of Jesus Christ; they are also our brothers and sisters because of him.

We'll begin this Mass by listening to what a few people who have lived in poor countries have said.

Gandhi said: 'The earth has enough for everyone's need, but not enough for everyone's greed.'

Niall O'Brien, an Irish priest in the Philippines, writes:
'The joint arms budget for 1987/88 has touched on 900 billion dollars. Enough to put food on the table daily of every hungry person in the world. Yet that money is set aside for death, to kill, to maim, to destroy, to create more hunger and destruction and frequently precisely to put down the revolutions caused by hunger, to silence the cry of the poor'.

Penitential Rite
With hope, we ask God's forgiveness for the inequality in the world.
> You came to your own people and they did not receive you:
> Lord have mercy.
> You died on the Cross for the sins of the world:
> Christ have mercy.
> You plead for us at God's right hand:
> Lord have mercy.

Opening Prayer
God our Father, deepen our conviction
that each man and woman in the world
is created in your image and likeness.
Help us all to work for the dignity of each person.
We make this prayer through Christ our Lord. Amen.

First Reading *Galatians 3:26-29*

> *In these lines Paul states that there are no distinctions of nationality or religion in the eyes of God. The same is true of wealth and poverty: all are children of God.*

A reading from the letter of Paul to the Galatians.

You are, all of you, children of God through faith in Jesus Christ. All baptized in Christ, you have all clothed yourselves in Christ, and there are no more distinctions between Jew and Greek, slave and free, male and female, but all of you are one in Christ Jesus.

Responsorial Psalm

Psalm 22 Prayer of people in great need.

RESPONSE: The Lord hears the cry of the poor; blessed be the Lord.

My God, my God, why have you forsaken me?
You are far from my prayer and the cry of my plea?
I call to you all the day long,
from my terrors set me free. R.

Do not stand aside, O Lord.
My strength, come quickly to my help;
rescue my soul from the sword,
then I will proclaim your name to my people,
praise you in the assembly of your people. R.

Gospel *Luke 2:6-8, 15-17*

> *We remember that at his birth Jesus was poor and homeless; in the lives of many millions of people he is still poor and homeless.*

A reading from the holy Gospel according to Luke.

While they were at Bethlehem, the time came for her to have her child, and she gave birth to a son, her first born. She wrapped him in swaddling clothes and laid him in a manger, because there was no room for them in the inn ... Now when the angels had gone from them into heaven, the shepherds said to one another, 'Let us go into Bethlehem and see this thing that has happened which the Lord has made known to us.' So they hurried away and found Mary and Joseph, and the baby lying in the manger.

Prayer of the Faithful

We pray for those who suffer from starvation; may those of us who have plenty be generous in our support of them; Lord, hear us.

We pray for people all over the world who are homeless, and ask God's blessing on all efforts to give people a home; Lord, hear us.

We pray for people who are in prison; Lord, hear us.

We pray for all those who work for the people of the Third World, for their efforts to create a better life for others, and ask that we be sensitive to injustice in our own country; Lord, hear us.

We ask that we can feel the pain that God feels at the tragedies of injustice, hunger and want in our world; Lord, hear us.

Let us pray:

God, give us eyes like yours, which see the want of the world,

a heart like yours, which hears the cry of innocent people,

and a willingness to do our best

to make things better for people in need.

We ask this through Christ our Lord. Amen.

Prayer over the Gifts

As we offer gifts of bread and wine,

may we also offer our own time and interest

in trying to help people in need.

We make this prayer through Christ our Lord. Amen.

Communion Reflection

Think of some faces of the world,

faces you have seen on the street of the city,

on the TV screen, or in the newspaper.

The woman nursing the starving child,

an old man evicted from a flat,

a young person imprisoned for protest against injustice,

the factory where kids of ten are working,

men and women walking for miles in the desert for food,

shanty towns as the rain sweeps hundreds of huts away,

refugees pushed from one place to another.

Jesus says:

whatever you do for my people, you do for me.

And whatever you fail to do for my people, you fail to do for me.

This means wherever people are hungry, I am hungry,

wherever people are homeless, I am homeless,

wherever people are exploited, I am exploited.

Gracious God, forgive us.
Loving God, make us feel for people as you feel.
Generous God, encourage us to help those in need.

Concluding Prayer
As we have received from this table, God our Father,
the food of life and the bread of our salvation,
we ask that we may become in our world
the compassion, forgiveness and justice of Jesus your Son,
who is Lord forever and ever. Amen.

35. Third World 2

Introduction

The subject of our Mass today is the Third World, with emphasis on the fact that many of the world's poor are kept poor, so that others can stay rich and get richer.

For example, much of what we use in the West is kept cheap by child labour in the factories of the third world. In cities, different social classes are kept apart by town planners. Some laws are a systematic way of keeping down a certain group of the population. The cost of education is a way of keeping education within the access only of some, and so the spiral of inequality goes on and on.

Let us ask God's forgiveness for the ways in which we live, which keep many nations and peoples poor and deprived. The oppressed and those who are poor are the special friends of God.

We need to become aware of systems of greed and how we take part in them. We ask at this Mass that we become sensitive to the ways in which people are suffering through no fault of their own, and to ways in which economic and political systems keep them down. And we pray that we may become increasingly aware that in the cry of every oppressed person – man, woman, or innocent child – we will hear the cry of Jesus in his people today.

Penitential Rite

We ask God's forgiveness and love in our lives, as we join in this Mass.
> Lord Jesus, you say that whatever we do to any of your people,
> we do to you:
> Lord have mercy.
> Lord Jesus, you have come to call the nations to repentance:
> Christ have mercy.
> Lord Jesus, you call us to generosity in your service from
> the throne of heaven:
> Lord have mercy.

Opening Prayer

God our Father, give us and all your church
a real desire for better conditions
for the millions of starving and poor people in the world.

Help us to be aware of their needs,
in our own country and in the whole world.
Grant this through Christ our Lord. Amen.

First Reading *Isaiah 1:10-17*

This is a harsh reading about God's reaction to sacrifices and prayers that don't also involve care for the needy.

A reading from the prophet Isaiah.

'What are your endless sacrifices to me?' says the Lord. 'I am sick of holocausts of rams and the fat of calves. Bring me your worthless offerings no more, the smoke of them fills me with disgust. New moons, sabbaths, assemblies, I cannot endure festival and solemnity. Your new moons and your pilgrimages I hate with all my soul. You may multiply your prayers, I shall not listen. Your hands are covered with blood; wash, make yourselves clean. Take your wrongdoing out of my sight. Cease to do evil, learn to do good, search for justice, help the oppressed, be just to the orphan, plead for the widow.

'Come now, let us talk this over', says the Lord. 'Though your sins are like scarlet, they shall be white as snow; though they are red as crimson, they shall be like wool.'

Responsorial Psalm

Psalm 94 A poem about the love of God for justice.
RESPONSE: The Lord is close to the brokenhearted.

You never consent to that corrupt tribunal
that imposes disorder as law,
and takes the life of the virtuous
and condemns the innocent to death. R.

No, the Lord is still my citadel,
my God is a rock where I take shelter;
he will pay them back for all their sins,
he will silence their wickedness. R.

Gospel *Luke 16:19-31*

This story is a serious reflection on the differences in our world. Lazarus is a symbol of the poor: Dives of the unsympathetic rich person. There is no doubt where Jesus' sympathy lies.

A reading from the holy Gospel according to Luke.

Jesus said to his disciples, 'There was a rich man who used to dress in purple and fine linen, and feasted magnificently every day. And at his gate there lay a poor man called Lazarus, covered with sores, who longed to fill himself with the scraps which fell from the rich man's table. Dogs even came and licked his sores. Now the poor man died and was carried away by the angels to the bosom of Abraham. The rich man also died and was buried.

In his torment in Hades he looked up and saw Abraham a long way off with Lazarus in his bosom. So he cried out, "Father Abraham, pity me and send Lazarus to dip the tip of his finger in water and cool my tongue, for I am in agony in these flames." "My son", Abraham replied, "remember that during your life good things came your way, just as bad things came the way of Lazarus. Now he is being comforted here while you are in great agony. But that is not all: between us and you a great gulf has been fixed to stop anyone crossing from your side to ours." The rich man replied, "Father, I beg you then to send Lazarus to my father's house, since I have five brothers, to give them warning so that they do not come to this place of torment, too." "They have Moses and the prophets," said Abraham "let them listen to them." "Ah no, Father Abraham," said the rich man, "but if someone comes to them from the dead they will repent." Then Abraham said to him, "If they will not listen either to Moses or the prophets, they will not be convinced even if someone should rise from the dead."'

Prayer of the Faithful
As a prayer of the faithful, prepare bowls of rice and pass them around to each person: this is the total food for a day for many millions of people in our world. Each person prays silently over the bowl of rice. Spontaneous intentions might be made at the end of the 'rice' prayer.

Prayer over the Gifts
Put some symbols of the suffering world on the altar: a cross of nails, a rice bowl, a crucifix, a syringe or medical object, and any other such symbols. Then say the following prayer.

Gracious God,
we offer these to you as gifts of our love for your people.
We offer them in sadness, in anger,
but in compassion and love.
As you come to us in bread and wine,

may you come to us also in justice for your people.
We ask this through Christ our Lord. Amen.

Communion Reflection
God, forgive us!
Forests, needed for the native economy in a debt-ridden third world nation have been cut down to give the raw material for food cartons to be cheaply made for the first world. God, forgive us.
Children of five and six are working ten hours or more a day in a hot factory of an Indian city to make profit for someone who never knows their conditions. God, forgive us.
A young man cannot go where he wants, work where he is qualified, all because of the colour of his skin. God, forgive us.
A city girl of sixteen is refused a job because she has the 'wrong address'. God, forgive us.
A woman is in prison for getting involved in the struggle for justice. God, forgive us.
Continue with spontaneous reflections for forgiveness.

Concluding Prayer
May we know ever more clearly, God our Father,
that you are especially close to us
when we suffer and when we work for those who suffer.
Give us hearts like yours,
that we may act justly,
love tenderly,
and walk humbly with you in our lives.
We ask this through Christ our Lord. Amen.

36. Care for Life

Introduction

Our theme for this Mass is care for life.

The best word to describe God's creation is life, and it is the most precious of gifts. People obviously go to great lengths to save, preserve, and cherish life. We would go to great lengths to save our own life; and, when we hear of someone whose burden of life was so great that he or she has committed suicide, we feel a great sympathy.

Life can also be treated cheaply: killings in war, violence in many parts of the world, kidnapping, imprisonment, abortion. These are ways in which human life is devalued and is looked on as having less than its real value.

Jesus valued life: he enjoyed the life of the earth, of all creation and, above all, treated each person with great dignity. He said he came on earth that 'we might have life and have it to the full'.

So we pray at this Mass that human life might be valued everywhere, and that we ourselves may always value life above all political, financial, and social concerns.

Penitential Rite

As we offer this Mass, we ask God's forgiveness for ways in which we have failed to value life as God does.

Lord Jesus, you come among us that we have life to the full:
Lord have mercy.
Lord Jesus, you give us the life of God in word and sacrament:
Christ have mercy.
Lord Jesus, you promise us life in God for all eternity:
Lord have mercy.

May almighty God have mercy on us, forgive us our sins, and bring us to life everlasting. Amen.

Opening Prayer

Gracious God, all life comes from you.
It is your gift to us.
In gratitude for the gift of life,
we pray that your people everywhere
may value each human life as precious in your eyes.

We ask this through Christ our Lord. Amen.

First Reading *Wisdom 11:24-12:1*
A title of God, often missed, is 'Lover of life'. Every living thing shares in the life of God.

A reading from the Book of Wisdom.

Lord, you love everything that exists, and nothing you have made disgusts you, since, if you hated something, you would not have made it. And how could a thing subsist, had you not willed it? Or how be preserved, if not called forth by you? No, you spare all, since all is yours, Lord, lover of life! For your imperishable spirit is in everything.

Responsorial Psalm
Psalm 34 A poem about the care God has for us.
RESPONSE: Lord, we thank you for the gift of life.

The eyes of the Lord are on those who revere him,
on those who rely on his love,
to rescue their souls from death,
and keep them alive in famine. R.

Our soul waits for the Lord,
he is our help and our shield;
our hearts rejoice in him,
we trust in his holy name.
Lord, let your love rest on us,
as our hope has rested in you. R.

Gospel *Luke 7:11-17*
Jesus valued the gift of life: he spoke of having life to the full. This story from the gospel is a sign of his wish that we, his people, be fully alive in love, in care, and in hope for ourselves and each other.
A reading from the holy Gospel according to Luke.

It happened soon afterwards he went to a town called Nain, accompanied by his disciples and a great number of people. Now when he was near the gate of the town there was a dead man being carried out, the only son of his mother, and she was a widow. And many of the townspeople were with her. When the Lord saw her he felt sorry for her and said to her, 'Don't cry.' Then he went up and touched the stretcher, and the bearers stood still, and he said, 'Young man, I tell you, get up.' And the dead man got up and began to talk. And Jesus gave him to his mother. Everyone was filled with awe and glorified God saying, 'A great prophet has risen up among us; God has visited his people.' And this view of him spread throughout Judaea and all over the countryside.

Prayer of the Faithful

As we pray about the gift of life, let us make our intentions to God:

Give us always, we pray, a love for life: for the life of the earth, for animal life, and above all for human life; Lord, hear us.

Forgive our sins against life; sins of violence, murder, abortion, and other ways in which we do not respect the gift of life; Lord, hear us.

For those who work in the service of life: for doctors, nurses, hospital staffs, especially in parts of the world where illness occurs through neglect of life and lack of food and water; Lord, hear us.

Help your people, Lord, to work for the fullness of life: that people everywhere may have enough to eat, to wear, and a home for their families; Lord, hear us.

Give eternal life to all who have died; Lord, hear us.

Let us pray:

God our Father, you are the source of life.

We ask that we may always be truly grateful for the gift of life, and see you as the God of all living things.

We ask this through Christ our Lord. Amen.

Presentation of the Gifts

Symbols of life are brought to the altar: e.g. plants, fish in a bowl (if appropriate), some earth with a flower in it, food, pictures of reconciliation, joy, love.

Prayer over the Gifts

God our Father, from the gifts of life you have given us, we now give you bread and wine.

We do this in thanks for all you have given us.

May they become the greatest of your gifts, the body and blood of Jesus our Lord. Amen.

Communion Reflection

Think of some pictures of life:

a father with a new born child,

a mother teaching her preschooler,
friends talking together,
a band playing music,
an honest conversation,
a moment of compassion.
All of these moments enable us to share in the life of God.
The glory of God is man and woman fully alive:
alive to the love among us,
alive to care and concern,
alive also in suffering, in pain and sorrow,
knowing that the life of God uplifts us.
God, thank you for the gift of life;
for the ways we bring each other alive,
for the ways we share physical life,
emotional support and spiritual hope.
Let us be, like you, lovers of life.

Concluding Prayer
We have received, loving God, the bread of life from this table.
May we always treasure and enjoy the gift of life,
and bring new life to those we meet.
We make this prayer through Christ our Lord. Amen.

37. Care for Society

Introduction
The theme of our readings at Mass today is our care for society.
We're thinking of the ways in which we live with other people in our cities, parishes, schools, workplaces. The question is, 'Can we make our society a better place, with more equality, less poverty, more tolerance, less discrimination, more peace, less violence?'

It's a tall order, but each person can make a difference. None of us, or indeed no group, has the full solution to the problems of society: the problems of loneliness, poverty, lack of faith, homelessness, unequal educational opportunities and many others; but all of us can be part of the solution.

Jesus made a difference to society by working for a change of heart in individuals and by calling for greater justice and equality.

We pray in this Mass that we may become more aware of the needs in our society, more ready to play some part in meeting them, and try to see them with the eyes of Jesus Christ.

Penitential Rite
We ask God's forgiveness for sin in our society, of which we are all a part.

Lord Jesus, you prayed for your enemies; forgive our sins of violence:
Lord have mercy.
Lord Jesus, you showed compassion and love to everyone; forgive our sins of intolerance:
Christ have mercy.
Lord Jesus, you plead for all your people at God's right hand; forgive our sins of coldness:
Lord have mercy.

Opening Prayer
Gracious God, you are present to your people always,
in all places, at every time.
Help us see your people with the eyes of Jesus.
Where there is injustice and inequality,
let us try to spread justice and equality;

help us to build a society
where each person is valued as a child of God
We ask this through Jesus Christ our Lord. Amen.

First Reading *James 2:14-17*

Faith is sincere when it results in action. If faith is strong, there will be activities going with it that make our society more Christian.

A reading from the letter of James.

How does it help, when someone who has never done a single good act claims to have faith? Will that faith bring salvation? If one of the brothers or one of the sisters is in need of clothes and has not enough food to live on, and one of you says to them, 'I wish you well; keep yourself warm and eat plenty', without giving them these bare necessities of life, then what good is that? In the same way faith: if good deeds do not go with it, it is quite dead.

Responsorial Psalm

Psalm 103 A poem about the compassion of God: real change in society comes from compassion for people.
RESPONSE: The Lord has compassion for his people.

The Lord is tenderness and pity,
slow to anger and rich in faithful love;
his indignation does not last forever,
nor his resentment remain for all time;
he does not treat us as our sins deserve,
nor repay us as befits our offenses. R.

The Lord's faithful love is from eternity and for ever;
and his saving justice to their children's children;
as long as they keep his covenant,
and carefully obey his commands. R.

Gospel *Matthew 9: 35-37*

Jesus' care for society is seen in his compassion for the suffering people of society. The Christian follower of Jesus sees society through the eyes of Jesus: people needing care, food, shelter, hope, faith, and love.

A reading from the holy Gospel according to Matthew.

Jesus made a tour through all the towns and villages, teaching in their synagogues, proclaiming the good news of the kingdom and curing all kinds of disease and all kinds of illness. And when he saw the crowds he felt sorry for them because they were harassed and dejected, like sheep without a shepherd. The he said to his disciples, 'The harvest is rich but the labourers are few, so ask the Lord of the harvest to send out labourers to his harvest'.

Prayer of the Faithful

We pray for the needs of our world: for a more loving and caring society and for a continuation of the work of Jesus in caring for society:

> Make us aware, Lord Jesus, of the need of so many people for food and shelter, for compassion and for hope; Lord, hear us.

> Make us aware, Lord Jesus, of your call to each of us to continue, in our own way, your care for society; Lord, hear us.

> We pray for people who spend their time in caring for the less fortunate, and for our own efforts on behalf of others; Lord, hear us.

Let us pray:
God our Father, creator of our world,
help us, in all our activities and plans,
to care for our society
in the Spirit of Jesus, your Son,
who is Lord forever and ever. Amen.

Prayer over the Gifts

Gracious God, use our hearts in your work of love
and our hands in your service of your people.
Make of us people who care for the society in which we live.
Grant this through Christ our Lord. Amen.

Communion Reflection

People wonder if their efforts to care for society are worth it.
Sheila Cassidy gave some years as a doctor in Chile.
Tortured, imprisoned, expelled, she wondered if her time was wasted.
From that question, she wrote her Credo:
'I believe no pain is lost,
no tear unmarked,
no cry of anguish dies unheard,
lost in the hail of gunfire or blanked out by the padded cell.
I believe that pain and prayer are somehow saved,
processed, stored, used in the Divine Economy.
The blood shed in Salvador will irrigate the heart

of some financier a million miles away.
The terror, pain, despair,
swamped by lava, flood or earthquake
will be caught up like mist and fall again,
a gentle rain on arid hearts
or souls despairing in the back streets of Brooklyn.'

Sheila Cassidy, Sharing the Darkness.

Concluding Prayer
Loving God, be with us as we leave this place of prayer
to spread your gospel in our society.
May we always co-operate with your care and interest in our world.
We ask this through Christ our Lord. Amen.

38. The Good Samaritan

Introduction

The story of the Good Samaritan, told by Jesus, is a story about love and compassion, especially to those most in need. It is the story of the homeless living in our streets, of young people who are insecure and lonely in a group, of a mother rearing a family on her own. It's a story about all of us at one time or another when we needed help, when we needed someone to pull us out of the ditch and someone came—or didn't come.

We'll be open now to that story of Jesus. Let it bring us to prayer and reflection on the world we live in, and pray that we may become people who are open to being helped and to helping others.

Penitential Rite

We call to mind now ways in which we have ignored the needs of others, or times when we were selfish in accepting help from others, and we ask Gods's forgiveness.

Lord, you are kind and compassionate to all your people:
Lord have mercy.
Lord, you came to seek out the lost and the sinner:
Christ have mercy.
Lord, you are our brother and our friend in the presence of God:
Lord have mercy.

Opening Prayer

God, Father and Creator of us all,
we come to you, in need of your help and presence.
We ask that we can be touched by the care of Christ your Son,
in the weakness and needs of our lives.
Make us sensitive to the cry of the poor,
the loneliness and the insecurity of people,
so that we share with them your compassion,
now and every day of our lives,
through Christ our Lord. Amen.

First Reading *Isaiah 55:1-3*

This is an invitation to come to God in all our needs so that our thirst for hope and meaning will be satisfied.

A reading from the prophet Isaiah.

O come to the water all you who are thirsty,
though you have no money, come.
Why spend money on what is not bread,
your wages on what fails to satisfy?
Listen, listen to me, and you will have good things to eat,
and rich food to enjoy.
Pay attention, come to me,
listen, and your soul will live.

Responsorial Psalm
Psalm 130 All who suffer cry to God for help and God hears our cries.
RESPONSE: The Lord hears the cry of the poor.

Out of the depths I cry to you, O Lord,
Lord, hear my voice.
O let your ears be attentive
to the voice of my pleading. R.

If you, O Lord, should mark our guilt,
Lord who would survive?
But with you is found forgiveness,
for this we revere you. R.

Because with the Lord there is mercy
and fullness of redemption.
Your people indeed you will redeem
from all our iniquity. R.

Gospel *Luke 10:29-37*
>   *The story of the Good Samaritan presents us with a person who helped*
>   *another in need, with a person who needed help and accepted it, and*
>   *with Jesus who himself is the Good Samaritan in his attitudes to his*
>   *people.*

A reading from the holy Gospel according to Luke.

A man said to Jesus, 'And who is my neighbour?' Jesus replied, 'A man
was once on his way from Jerusalem to Jericho and fell into the hands
of brigands; they took all he had, beat him and then made off, leaving
him half dead. Now a priest happened to be travelling down the same
road, but he saw the man and passed by on the other side. In the same
way a Levite who came to the place saw him, and passed by on the
other side. But a Samaritan traveller who came upon him bandaged his

wounds, pouring oil and wine on them. He then lifted him onto his own mount, carried him to the inn and looked after him. Next day he took out two denarii and handed them to the innkeeper. 'Look after him', he said 'and on my way back I will make good any extra expense you have.' 'Which of these three, do you think, proved himself a neighbour to the man who fell into the brigands' hands?' 'The one who took pity on him,' he replied. Jesus said to him, 'Go, and do the same yourself.'

Prayer of the Faithful

We remember people and places in our world that remind us of this story and we pray for them. We pray, too, for our own sensitivity to the needs of others.

For people who suffer through violence and through robbery, especially the old who live in fear and for those who are without father or mother through war and violence:
Response: Lord, in your compassion, hear our prayer.
For the innocent who suffer, for children who are born into extreme poverty, for the poor whose needs are exploited by the greed of others: Lord hear us. R.
That we may be sensitive to the needs of others, particularly of the less fortunate in our country, and act in our own lives like good Samaritans: Lord hear us. R.

God our Father, we pray to you to hear the needs
of your people. Help us to see in Christ your care and love for us, and to hear in him your call to help the needy.
We ask this in his name. Amen.

Invitation to Communion

This is the Lamb of God, the Bread of Life. This is the gift of God to all of us in our need and our weakness. This is our sign that we are called to care for others, and we are happy to be called to this Eucharist.
Lord, I am not worthy to receive you,
but only say the word and I shall be healed.

Communion Reflection

I wonder about the man who fell among the robbers,
a poor man, mugged, robbed of money, thrown in a ditch.
What were his feelings as he lay in the ditch?
Was he afraid—with a terrible fear—that nobody cared?

And then when someone did come? What meant most to him?
The ointment touched gently onto his broken skin,
or the voice speaking gently to his broken spirit?
The Samaritan traveller was more than a helping hand.
He offered compassion and care to the broken man
and a promise that he would return to see how he was.

What meant most?
Probably the touch that went with the soothing hand,
the touch that restored his feeling of human dignity,
the touch that told him he mattered.
That's the touch of Christ.

Concluding Prayer
God our Father, bless us as we go;
we are sent forth into our world
to notice its needs and respond as we can.
Give us a heart like your Son's
open in sympathy and compassion
and touching everyone with his belief
in the immense worth of each person.
We thank you for this belief
in Christ our Lord. Amen.

39. The Breaking of Bread

Introduction

We live in a world of signs. A ring on a finger means a person is married, a light in a dark house is a sign that someone is at home. Handshakes are signs of greeting and friendship. A flag is a sign of a nation.

Jesus wanted to leave a sign of his presence among us, for he is risen to eternal life with his Father. He told us that whenever his friends meet and break bread – a human sign of companionship and fellowship – he would be present. The reason he chose bread is its simplicity and its homeliness. It is the work of human hands, an essential of our life. He chose it also because it represents the fact that his body was broken for us, his whole life was poured out for us.

The breaking of bread which happens at every Mass is a sign of God's presence here and now, and also a challenge to us to share our lives with God's people. That's what we'll be praying and thinking about at this Mass.

Penitential Rite

We come to God for forgiveness and for strength to live our lives in a Christian way. When we break bread and receive Jesus in the Eucharist, we commit ourselves to live like he did. We have confidence that with his help we can do that.

> Lord, you are known in the breaking of bread:
> Lord have mercy.
> Lord, you give us yourself in the bread of life:
> Christ have mercy.
> Lord, you are present with us here and at the right hand of God:
> Lord have mercy.

Opening Prayer

Gracious God, be with us,
our inspiration in all we say and do.
As your Son gave a sign of his presence in the breaking of bread,
may we be his presence in the world
in how we relate to others,
and in all we say and do.
We ask this in his name. Amen.

First Reading *1 Corinthians 11:23-27*
> *When Christians meet, they do what the Lord Jesus did: pray, give thanks, and receive the bread of life, broken in the death of Christ. This is Paul's message.*

A reading from the first letter of Paul to the Corinthians.

For this is what I received from the Lord, and in turn passed on to you: that on the same night that he was betrayed, the Lord Jesus took some bread and thanked God for it and broke it, and he said, 'This is my body, which is for you; do this as a memorial of me.' In the same way he took the cup after supper, and said, 'This cup is the new covenant in my blood. Whenever you drink it, do this as a memorial to me.' Until the Lord comes, therefore, every time you eat this bread and drink this cup, you are proclaiming his death, and so anyone who eats the bread or drinks the cup of the Lord unworthily will be behaving unworthily towards the body and blood of the Lord.

Responsorial Psalm
Psalm 23 The writer of the psalm believes that God is always near to help us.
RESPONSE: We thank you, Lord, for this bread of life.

The Lord is my shepherd;
there is nothing I shall want.
Fresh and green are the pastures
where he gives me repose.
Near restful waters he leads me,
to revive my drooping spirit. R

He guides me along the right path;
he is true to his name.
If I should walk in the valley of darkness
no evil would I fear.
You are there with your crook and your staff;
with these you give me comfort. R.

You have prepared a banquet for me
in the sight of my foes.
My head you have anointed with oil;
my cup is overflowing. R.

Gospel Luke 7:18-22
> *In the Gospel Jesus tells us how he 'breaks bread' in real life: healing*

the sick, encouraging the anxious, forgiving the sinner.

A reading from the holy Gospel according to Luke.

The disciples of John gave him all this news, and John, summoning two of his disciples, sent them to Jesus to ask, 'Are you the one who is to come, or must we wait for someone else?' When the men reached Jesus they said, 'John the Baptist has sent us to you, to ask, "Are you the one who is to come or have we to wait for someone else?"' It was just then that he cured many people of diseases and afflictions and of evil spirits, and gave the gift of sight to many who were blind. Then he gave the messengers their answer, 'Go back and tell John what you have seen and heard: the blind can see again, the lame walk, lepers are cleansed, and the deaf hear, the dead are raised to life, the Good News is proclaimed to the poor and happy are those who do not lose faith in me.'

Prayer of the Faithful
We pray to God, remembering particularly the needs of people we know who need both our prayers and our help in their lives.
> For the sick and the dying, for people who are in any way handicapped or disabled and for those who look after them; that they may find the care of the Lord in their troubles:
> *Response: Lord, you gave your life for us, hear our prayers.*
> That all of us, and all your followers, will be sincere in our Christian life, that when we break bread and receive communion, we'll show in our lives our faith in Christ: Lord hear us. R.
> We remember our own families and friends, and we ask you to bless those who are kind to us: Lord hear us. R.

We pray, loving God, that your church and all your people
will be instruments of your peace and concern.
Give us the courage we need to follow Jesus,
so that our relationships may reflect his care and your love.
We ask this in his name. Amen.

Prayer over the Gifts
Accept our gifts, God, we pray,
and give us the courage of Jesus, your Son,
who has come among us
to be your love of the poor and the deprived in our world.
As this bread is food for all your people
so may our hearts be open

to spread your justice and love in our world.
We ask this in the name of Christ the Lord. Amen.

Invitation to Communion
This is the bread of life, broken by our cruelty and injustice, restored
by the power of God which raised Jesus to life. We are happy to be
called to this Eucharist.
Lord I am not worthy to receive you,
but only say the word and I shall be healed.

Communion Reflection
Too many people live in misery because nobody knows
and too many are in darkness because nobody cares.
Old people alone, in squalor – need this be?
Travellers in the rain of weather and unconcern?
Third world starvation when there is a grain surplus?
The powerful nations invading the small
to protect commercial interests?
God's people need the bread of life,
of concern, compassion, care.
God needs us to make and break this bread,
to shape and share it,
to give it to others and to receive it back again.

Concluding Prayer
Loving God, by sharing in the bread of life,
we are brought into community with all your people.
We pray that we can be men and women for others,
open in our hearts and using our talents
in building a world more equal in the sharing of its resources,
more loving to all its people
and more concerned with the dignity of all your people.
We make this prayer in the name of Christ the Lord. Amen.

40. Heart for Justice

Introduction
Our television screens bring the starvation and homelessness of the 'third world' into our homes. We are horrified by scenes of famine and disaster. We know and yet we don't know: these people are near to us and yet far away.

The world of the Gospel was something like this. The heart of Jesus was stretched to its limits of friendship and compassion by the hundreds of sick, crippled, and injured people he met. He was so close to them that he felt their suffering deeply, for that's what love means.

He still suffers in his people; he is hungry in Africa, homeless in India, oppressed in the shanty towns of South America. He works also for his people in hearts which are open to the cries of the oppressed, and in the efforts made by others on their behalf. That's the theme of our reflection and prayer today as we offer Mass. We try to see how Jesus himself reacts and challenges us in the cry for justice.

Penitential Rite
The misery of many millions of people is the fault of other millions. We ask forgiveness now for our world, because the systems we live in cause so much heartbreak and hopelessness, hunger and homelessness to so many people.

> Lord Jesus, you said that what we do for our brothers and sisters on earth, we do for you:
> Lord have mercy.
> Lord Jesus, you have come that we may have life and have it to the full:
> Christ have mercy.
> Lord Jesus, you are raised from death by the love of God:
> Lord have mercy.

Opening Prayer
Gracious God, we pray that you may be a light in the darkness of our world:
we ask you that in the light you share with us,
we become aware of the needs of your people:
see the faces marred by frustration;
feel the thirst for justice;

be burned by the desire to care for each other.
We make this prayer through Christ our Lord. Amen.

First Reading *Isaiah 58:5-9*
   This is a reading linking our work for the oppressed with the light of God.

A reading from the prophet Isaiah.

Hanging your head like a reed,
lying down on sackcloth and ashes?
Is that what you call fasting,
a day acceptable to the Lord?

Rather, this the sort of fast that pleases me
– it is the Lord who speaks –
to break unjust fetters
and undo the thongs of the yoke,

to let the oppressed go free,
and break every yoke,
to share your bread with the hungry,
and shelter the homeless poor,

to clothe the naked
and not turn from your own kin?
Then will your light shine like the dawn
and your wound be quickly healed over.

Your integrity will go before you
and the glory of the Lord behind you.
Cry, and the Lord will answer;
call, and he will say, 'I am here'.

Responsorial Psalm
Psalm 86 A poem and prayer in our weakness.
RESPONSE: The Lord hears the cry of the poor.

Turn your ear, O Lord, and give answer
for I am poor and needy.
Preserve my life, for I am faithful:
save the servant who trusts in you. R.

You are my God, have mercy on me, Lord,
for I cry to you all the day long.
Give joy to your servant, O Lord,

for to you I lift up my soul. R.

O Lord, you are good and forgiving,
full of love to all who call.
Give heed, O Lord, to my prayer
and attend to the sound of my voice. R.

Gospel *Matthew 15:29-37*

Jesus looks on many oppressed people and feeds them. His response is to open his heart to help them in whatever way he can. The food he shares is also the food of the Eucharist, which challenges us to be like him, open-hearted for justice.

A reading from the holy Gospel according to Matthew.

Jesus went on from there and reached the shores of the Sea of Galilee, and he went up into the hills. He sat there and large crowds came to him, bringing the lame, the crippled, the blind, the dumb and many others; these they put down at his feet, and he cured them. The crowds were astonished to see the dumb speaking, the lame walking, and the blind with their sight, and they praised the God of Israel. But Jesus called his disciples to him and said, 'I feel sorry for all these people; they have been with me for three days now and have nothing to eat. I do not want to send them off hungry, they might collapse on the way.' The disciples said to him, 'Where could we get enough bread in this deserted place to feed such a crowd?' Jesus said to them, 'How many loaves have you?' 'Seven,' they said, 'and a few small fish.' Then he instructed the crowd to sit down on the ground, and he took the seven loaves and the fish, and he gave thanks and broke them and handed them to the disciples who gave them to the crowds. They all ate as much as they wanted, and they collected what was left of the scraps, seven baskets full. Now four thousand had eaten, to say nothing of women and children.

Prayer of the Faithful

We pray now, after thinking about the needs of the developing world, after hearing how Jesus himself would respond. We pray also for the needs of our own country.

Response: Lord hear our prayer.

We ask forgiveness for the greed of our world, for the selfishness of the developed world and the ways it gets richer on the needs of the poor. Lord hear us. R.

Help us, too, to see the inequalities between rich and poor at home, to be sensitive to those in need, and to do what we can in public and in private to help your people who need our help: Lord hear us. R.

For leaders of churches and of state, for our own political leaders: we pray that the needs of the poor and oppressed will be heard in the legislation of our country and in the preaching of the Gospel: Lord hear us. R.

God our Father, you ask us in your word
to love tenderly, act justly and walk humbly with you, our God.
You have been like this to us,
to each person your Son met in his life on earth.
Help us to be like him in all we do,
for he is Lord forever and ever. Amen.

Prayer over the Gifts
Our gifts, loving God, are small
but valued signs of our friendship with you,
and of your friendship with us.
Receive them and deepen within us
the desire to be friends with you,
through Jesus Christ our Lord. Amen.

Invitation to Communion
The bread of life is the gift of God for everyone. We are all equal in his sight, brothers and sisters of Jesus. We are happy to be called to this Eucharist.
Lord, I am not worthy to receive you,
but only say the word and I shall be healed.

Communion Reflection
When I was hungry you gave me food,
and when I was thirsty you refreshed me;
I was lonely and you gave me your time,
homeless, and you tried to put a roof over my head;
I was the victim of violence and greed
and you fought for my rights,
I was a refugee and you took me in.
'When, Lord?, when?' we will say,
because we never see you, nor do we know you suffer still.
We wonder at so much inequality in the world,
and it makes us angry, frustrated, helpless.

Sometimes you don't seem to be of much help,
remote, outside it all, and we say,
'Why didn't you make it all different?'
'When, Lord, when?' we will say,
and all you say, with a tear in your voice and hope in your heart,
'What you did for them, you did for me'.

Concluding Prayer
Bless each person here, God our Father, before we go.
Bless our good desires to serve you,
to live our lives according to our convictions.
As we gather here in the name of Jesus Christ
may we be strengthened to live in his name. Amen.

Of Related Interest...

50 Children's Liturgies for All Occasions
Francesca Kelly
Appealing themes, such as Sharing, Trust, Friends are a Gift, and Talents are explored and supported by appropriate original prayers and Scripture readings.

ISBN: 0-89622-541-0, 192 pp, $9.95

Lectionary for Masses with Children
Sean McEntee
Each Sunday's readings are preceded by a short dramatization that highlights the key elements for children.

Year A: ISBN: 0-89622-411-2, 216 pp, $19.95
Year B: ISBN: 0-89622-435-x, 216 pp, $19.95
Year C: ISBN: 0-89622-385-x, 152 pp, $19.95

Preaching and Teaching the Gospels to Children
Sean McEntee
The author helps readers through a simple teaching process, offering an overview of the Sunday readings and how to communicate its meaning to children. Included are simple actions to further help children understand the Gospel.

Year A: ISBN: 0-89622-524-0, 152 pp, $9.95
Year B: ISBN: 0-89622-569-0, 168 pp, $9.95
Year C: ISBN: 0-89622-491-0, 192 pp, $9.95

Available at religious bookstores or from
TWENTY-THIRD PUBLICATIONS
P.O. Box 180 • Mystic, CT 06355
1-800-321-0411